A Collector's Guide to the
SAVAGE 99 RIFLE
and its Predecessors, the Models 1895 and 1899

DAVID ROYAL

Photographs by Charlotte Royal

Edited by Rick Edmonds

Schiffer Publishing Ltd

4880 Lower Valley Road • Atglen, PA 19310

Dedication

To my wife, Merris. Before I started writing this book, my wife put up with me attending numerous collector gun shows, enduring interminable conversations between myself and other Model 99 enthusiasts. Things went downhill after I started the book. She then had to endure lengthy photography sessions and conversations that went into the deepest and—to her—the most boring aspects of the subject. She also had to put up with my inattentiveness, forgetfulness, and grouchiness during the actual writing of the book, not to mention living in an uncompleted remodeling project.

Cover design by Justin Watkinson
Type set in Helvetica, Eurostile & Minion

ISBN: 978-0-7643-5026-9

Printed in the United States

Published by Schiffer Publishing, Ltd.
4880 Lower Valley Road
Atglen, PA 19310
Phone: (610) 593-1777; Fax: (610) 593-2002
E-mail: Info@schifferbooks.com

For our complete selection of fine books on this and related subjects, please visit our website at www.schifferbooks.com. You may also write for a free catalog.

This book may be purchased from the publisher. Please try your bookstore first.

We are always looking for people to write books on new and related subjects. If you have an idea for a book, please contact us at proposals@schifferbooks.com.

Schiffer Publishing's titles are available at special discounts for bulk purchases for sales promotions or premiums. Special editions, including personalized covers, corporate imprints, and excerpts can be created in large quantities for special needs. For more information, contact the publisher.

CONTENTS

FOREWORD

The American firearms industry is truly remarkable and unique in the world. Strong-minded and innovative men coupled with superior manufacturing technologies have created refined firearms that have purpose, reliability, and firepower. Beginning in the late 1800s, hunters and shooters have enjoyed affordable firearms that were designed with their specific needs in mind, creating a multi-billion dollar industry that is still thriving today.

One of those individuals that carved a special place in firearm history is Arthur Savage—and not just in the firearms industry. He was a pioneer in many commercial markets, from farming to automobile tires. But he was perhaps best known for single-handedly developing the Model 99 rifle, originally known as the Model 1895. Truly innovative, practical, and superior to any lever action rifle of its era, the Model 99 is an eloquent expression of form and function.

As CEO of Savage, I was often frustrated with the lack of coherent history on that particular firearm, especially as I used an earlier 99 in .308 on all manner of game, from moose to coyotes.

I first met David and Merris Royal when they visited the Savage factory in Westfield, Massachusetts. They toured our museum lobby and remarked on certain firearms with unusual clarity and obvious experience. I was impressed with David's knowledge and passion, and more so when I found out he was an ex-marine, a talented photographer, an extra in a number of notable movies, and had a background in restoring Harley Davidson and Indian motorcycles. It soon became obvious he was not just a casual observer of firearm history, but was immersed in it and totally enamored with the Model 99.

I completely understand the fascination.

Being mechanically minded and inquisitive, David is uniquely qualified to fully explore the history of the Model 99 from its conception in 1893 to its numerous incarnations, culminating in 1995 with the centennial Model 99 in .300 Savage.

While I mourn the passing of this great product, I am reminded that it served its owners well for over a century and will continue to be a prime example of early American ingenuity for perhaps another century.

Savage Arms toyed with reintroducing the Model 99 in 2000, but after a year of study and testing decided the manufacturing cost of such a complex piece of machinery that would remain true to the original design was not economically feasible, especially as it was limited to the .308 caliber. The back of the bolt body on the action was cut at a four degree angle to facilitate a soft closing and anything more powerful than a .308 would push the bolt backwards and downward, creating excessive headspace.

This book chronicles a century of models, calibers, and permutations of a classic firearm, one that spawned numerous features in future designs by other manufacturers. All original technology is eventually superseded, but hopefully not without recognition for the originator.

David started hunting with the Savage lever action at the age of thirteen, and that positive experience led to his becoming an avid user and collector. His in-depth study of the history of 99s provides the reader with invaluable details from prototypes to the last production model.

Exploring little known subjects like Savage's only production military lever action rifle—the Montreal Home Guard musket— and the lightweight Perris Special, David uses photographs and information sources from all over the nation to reconstruct this fascinating firearm. He is diligent in his search for facts and substance and assembled an easy-to-follow history lesson that firearm enthusiasts will surely appreciate.

This book celebrates a man, his legacy, and our unique heritage as Americans—firearms being an extension of our personalities and fondness for superior tools.

And thanks to David, we now have a better appreciation for a firearm well ahead of its time, the Savage Model 99.

Ronald Coburn
New Hampshire
November 30, 2014

PREFACE

It is amazing to me that this book has not been written by someone else in the eleven or so years since the end of production of the Savage Model 99 rifle. Some of the reasons this is amazing are the following:

- The Savage Model 1895—the first version of this fine rifle—launched the Savage Arms Company, which in the 1920s and '30s produced the largest variety of firearms of any manufacturer in the world.
- Since 1895 Savage has sold over eighty million firearms.
- Savage produced the largest number of center fire rifles of any manufacturer in the United States last year (2013).
- Over a million Savage Model 1895, 1899, and 99s were sold over its 108-year production run.
- It was incredibly innovative at the time it was introduced and people still marvel at its design.
- It is an extremely beautiful and sleek rifle.
- There is a lot of collector interest in the various Models.

Douglas Murray wrote *The Ninety-Nine*, which was first published in 1977 and last updated in 1985. This is a great guide to the subject and started many people, including myself, collecting these rifles. It is black and white and used photos and information gleaned from Savage catalogs and observations of as many Model 99s as Doug could locate. Unfortunately, there are some errors in the catalogs that Doug repeated in his book. These errors are understandable, since the catalogs were the best source of information available to Doug in the age before the internet. In defense of Savage's catalogs, the era we are talking about did not have the quick turnaround time now available to publish time-sensitive material like catalogs, so the reality is the design and manufacture of the actual firearm would sometimes evolve after the catalog was printed. Catalogs are only a brief guide to what will be available and can't go into fine details of the product. *The Ninety-Nine* also does not go into a great deal of detail on the various models. I have attempted to go into much more detail based on observations of the rifles by other people and myself and have added information and photos on the Montreal Home Guard musket and the Model 99s produced from 1986 to 2003 that are not covered in *The Ninety-Nine*.

I am fortunate to have had access to the "24 Hour Campfire Savage Forum." There are a large number of people using the forum who have access to thousands of Savage Models 1895, 1899, and 99 who are willing to share information with the public. While my knowledge of these rifles was extensive when I decided to write the book, it is much greater now thanks to this forum and the opportunities provided me by a number of collectors who allowed me to visit them and view and photograph their rifles.

ACKNOWLEDGMENTS

First and foremost, I want to thank Rick Edmonds for making his encyclopedic knowledge of the Savage Model 99 rifles available to me. I also want to thank him for editing the book for content and believing I was capable of writing the book. He also provided several of the tables.

I also want to thank Ronald Coburn, Albert Kasper, and the Savage factory for their wholehearted support of the book and allowing me to photograph the prototypes at the factory.

My niece, Charlotte Royal, took the majority of the photographs and treated all of the photographs and diagrams.

Cheryl Johnson provided a number of photographs of her husband Don Johnson's collection of Model 99s.

Don Johnson, Dick Johnson, Doug Foglio, Darrell Russell, John Wright, Bill McNally, and Rick Edmonds allowed me to visit their homes and photograph their collections and gave me invaluable information on the 99s.

Rick Ruetten hosted Savage Fest 2014, which gave Charlotte and me the opportunity to photograph rifles belonging to him, Steve Balleck, Rory Reynoldson, Bruce Bacon, and Max Parduhn, plus additional rifles owned by Rick Edmonds and John Wright that I did not photograph during my earlier visits.

Gary Groshel provided vintage photos of people with their Savage rifles.

Bailey Brower and Luke Mercaldo let me use information from their books.

Savage historian John T. Callahan gave me input on Savage production dates and valuable information on my various rifles that I incorporated into the book.

The Buffalo Bill Cody Firearms Museum for allowing me to photograph their Savage rifles.

James D. Julia, Inc., auctions, Fairfield, Maine, for letting me use their photos of engraved Savage 1899s.

My brother's wife, Cathy Royal, and their daughter Crista for editing the book for grammar, spelling, and style.

INTRODUCTION

Part of the title of this book is "A Collector's Guide." My goal was to write a book that a collector or potential collector could refer to as a guide for their interest in the Savage Model 99 firearms family. This book should fill that need whether the collector is a neophyte or advanced and whether his or her interest is limited to one model or all of them. The book goes into great detail about each model, offers comparisons between models, and covers changes that came about during the production run of the models that did change. Some of the models did not change, many had minor changes, and one went through changes to the point that the final variation bears only a slight resemblance to the first.

The book is written pretty much in chronological order. The subject does not fit perfectly into this order, and in some cases I covered a model completely in one place, even though it overlapped into the next section or chapter; in other cases I covered later variations of the model in the appropriate section because the information seemed to fit better there.

Like everything that is produced over a long period of time, the Savage Model 99 evolved to meet the needs and desires of the firearms' buying public, adapted to changes in manufacturing technology, and handled more powerful ammunition that became available over the production run of the rifle.

I got my first Savage 99 in 1958, but I did not start seriously collecting these rifles until 2005. Even though I only had a few Model 99s in 2006, I decided I needed to take them to collector gun shows and share them with other people. This was a steep learning curve for me, and there were many people I met at the gun shows and continued to network with. It helped give me the knowledge to develop a coherent collection and indicated that a new book on the subject was needed. I then became active on the "24 Hour Campfire Savage Forum," further increasing my conviction that a new book was needed. I suggested to several people who are more knowledgeable than me that they should write a new book on the Model 99. They declined to write the book themselves, but agreed to share their knowledge with me if I would write it. I went into this endeavor with the conviction that the book must be written, but also that my knowledge was somewhat limited, that I had to do a lot of field work, and that I needed to access the knowledge of a lot of other people and pull it all into a coherent whole.

It is very difficult to photograph curved shiny surfaces. Photographers have dulling spray available that is easily removed with water. Using water on collectable firearms was not an option for us. We manipulated the lighting to eliminate reflections in critical curved places, such as barrel addresses and engraving. In some cases the result is the bluing appears grayer than its actual color.

I was very fortunate to visit the factory and meet Ronald Coburn early in the writing of this book. Ron had recently retired as Savage's CEO and oversaw the end of Model 99 production during his tenure. Having access to the prototypes and being able to talk to Ron in the early stages and as the book progressed has been very valuable. The collectors who let me visit with them, photograph their rifles and related material, and pick their brains contributed immeasurably to the book and are listed in the acknowledgments.

I have thoroughly enjoyed writing this book and hope that the reader will find it informative and enlightening.

David Royal

Chapter 1

ARTHUR W. SAVAGE AND HIS PROTOTYPES

Arthur W. Savage

A Short Note about Arthur Savage, the Inventor of the Savage Lever Action Rifle and Founder of Savage Arms

Arthur W. Savage was one of those brilliant individuals who embraced a new endeavor, made a success of it, then moved on to something else. His most notable achievement was inventing the Savage lever action rifle that became best known as the Savage Model 99 and established the Savage Arms Company that is still thriving today.

There were actually three production models of this rifle: the Model 1895, produced from 1895 until 1898; the Model 1899, produced from late 1898 until about 1923; and the Model 99, produced from about 1923 until 2003. These rifles evolved from the prototypes below.

A. W. Savage was a British citizen born in Jamaica in 1857 to a British government official. He was educated in Britain and the US as a Christian missionary and an artist. After some successful adventures in Australia he returned to Jamaica in 1885. In 1883, the British government announced it wanted a repeating rifle based on the single shot Martini. Savage started working on this idea in 1886, possibly before he left Jamaica. Savage's life took a dramatic turn in 1886, when he moved to New York and went to work for Munn & Company, a publisher of scientific papers, patents, and magazines. This seems to have sparked his inventive genius; as far as is known he had not shown any inclination for inventing prior to his interest in the Martini repeater.

While at Munn & Company he also patented the Savage-Halpine torpedo, which he improved from Halpine's original design. By 1887, he had patented the Martini repeater (**figures 1-1 through 1-3**). Next he moved to Utica, NY, and became the manager of Utica's run-down belt line railroad. His managerial skills turned it into a profitable operation. During this time he was working at night on firearms development. By late 1904, he was working on a cotton picking machine. In 1905, he was let go as managing director, sold at least part of his interest in the company, and moved to California, where he bought an orange grove. In 1911, he moved to San Diego and patented and started producing a new and improved pneumatic automobile tire. He worked further on firearms design with his son, Arthur J. Savage, did some painting, and established a ceramics company. For a detailed account of Arthur W. Savage's life see *Savage Pistols* by Bailey Brower Jr.[1]

Figure 1-1. Arthur Savage's first lever action repeater (serial #1) was a Martini-based repeater in 45-70 Government caliber.

Figure 1-2. Closeup of the action of Arthur Savage's first lever action rifle.

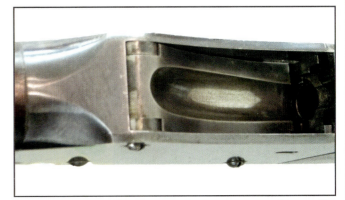

Figure 1-3. The top of the receiver with the lever open on Savage rifle number 1.

Arthur Savage's First rifle, the Martini-based Repeater

Arthur Savage's earliest attempt at a small arm was adapting a British Martini single shot to a repeater. The first rifle had a four-shot tubular magazine in the buttstock and was chambered in 45-70 government caliber (**see figures 1-1, 1-2, and 1-3, taken at the James D. Julia auction in March 2013**). The only marking on this rifle is the number 1. Figure 1-4 shows another version of this rifle that is in the Savage Arms Company's museum. (Figures 1-4 to 1-20 were taken at the Savage factory by Charlotte Royal and the author in March 2014.) Note that it features a closed loop lever and a sporter type forearm. The action in this rifle is obviously somewhat different than Savage number 1, as the lever hinges in front to the trigger. There are no visible markings on this rifle. A later design had its magazine in the breechblock, but proved to be too complicated and Savage abandoned the Martini project. It is doubtful any of these rifles were produced.

Figure 1-4. The Savage factory's Martini-based repeater. Note the closed loop lever and sporting type fore end.

The Model 1892 Prototype

Savage turned next to an entirely new design that he developed for submission to the Magazine Gun Board of the US Army Ordnance Department rifle trials convened in December 1890. These rifles were probably produced by Colt. It was a hammerless design with a rotary magazine similar to the Mannlicher design of 1887. It had an eight-round magazine capacity that resulted in a wide, deep receiver that protruded below the lever boss. The rear of the bolt was "T"-shaped and mated to a "T"-shaped opening in the receiver. One of the government's requirements was that it have a cartridge counter (**see Fig. 1-8**). It was chambered in .30 US Government (30-40 Krag) and was patented in 1892. The barrel is 33in long and the overall feel is rather cumbersome. The army chose the 1892 Krag rifle as the new military repeater over the Savage, despite the fact that the Krag did not have the cartridge counter. There are no visible markings on this rifle (**see Figures 1-5 through 1-9**).

Figure 1-5. Overall photo of Savage 1892 patent musket at the Savage factory.

Figure 1-6. Top view of the 1892 musket showing the T-shaped rear mating surface of the bolt.

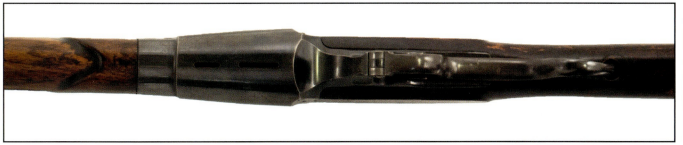

Figure 1-7. Bottom view of the 1892 musket showing milled slots that would allow water to drain out of the action.

Figure 1-8. The 1892 musket with the lever open. Note the bulging lower receiver. The hole near the lower front of the receiver is the cartridge counter. This is a feature that was carried forward on most models until 1985.

Figure 1-9. The 1892 musket with the lever open. Note the T-shaped receiver area that mates to the bolt.

The Model 1893 Prototype

Savage next designed a much smaller rifle using the basic design of the 1892 patent rifle. Colt was involved in the design of this rifle and may have produced it. The magazine capacity was reduced to five rounds, making it possible for the bottom of the receiver to form a smooth line from the forearm back to the lever boss (**compare figures 1-8 and 1-10**). The 1893 was chambered in 32-20 Winchester. The T-shaped bolt and receiver mating surface were changed to a simpler square design (**see Fig. 1-13**). This rifle was patented in 1893 and became the basis for the design of the production model 1895. It is much smaller and lighter than the 1892 patent rifle and the Model 1895. For example, the loading/ejection opening in the receiver is only 2.0875 inch, compared to an 1895 with a 3.288 inch opening. In my opinion Savage should have produced this rifle in calibers 25-20, 32-20, 38-40, and 44-40 to compete with Winchester's Model 1892. It would have been a great companion piece to the larger 1895/1899 high-power rifle. Savage designed this rifle with the intent to market it for civilian consumption, which probably explains the fine checkering (**see Figures 1-10 to 1-15**). Arthur Savage then refined this design into the model 1895.

Figure 1-10. Overall view of the 1893 prototype.

Figure 1-11. Top view of the 1893 prototype action with the lever closed.

Figure 1-12. Bottom view of the 1893 prototype action.

Figure 1-13. The action open on the 1893 prototype.

Figure 1-14. Forearm checkering and the cartridge counter on the 1893 prototype.

Figure 1-15. The checkering on the 1893 prototype stock.

The Pre-1899 Military Rifle

Here is another prototype that the factory tag identifies as a "Pre-1899 Savage lever action military test model" (**figures 1-16 through 1-20**). The barrel is 28.25in long and the receiver is larger than the 1895 and 1899 in almost all dimensions. The length of the receiver compared to an 1895 is about one-half inch longer. The loading/ejection opening is about three-quarters of an inch longer. The width of the receiver at the front is about the same and the width at the rear of the taper even with the back of the bolt is about one-sixteenth inch wider. Notice the sides of the receiver bulge are somewhat like the 1892 prototype (**compare figures 1-17 and 1-20 to figures 1-8 and 1-9**). I wonder if the factory mislabeled this rifle and it is actually a transition rifle from the 1892/1893 prototypes to the 1895. However,

the bolt has the 1899 cocking indicator; the bolt is too long to be one of the replacement 1895 rectangular cocking indicator bolts offered after the introduction of the 1899 (**see chapter 2, page 29 for details on these replacement bolts**). There is no indication what caliber the rifle is. It is possibly an 1899 prototype chambered in .30-40 Krag and the larger receiver was necessary for that chambering. Updated information strongly suggests that this rifle was developed for the New York National Guard trials in 1896. (see page 22 for more information on these trials).

There were two other prototypes at the factory: an early takedown (covered in chapter 3) and a 30-06 caliber rifle (covered in chapter 6) with the other rifles produced in the 1930s.

Figure 1-16. The Savage factory pre-1899 military test rifle.

Figure 1-17. Pre-1899 military rifle. Note the handguard, military ladder sight, and early 1899-type rectangular cocking indicator on the bolt. The production 1895 and 1899 military muskets did not have the handguard (see Figures 2-6 and 3-2).

Figure 1-18. Pre-1899 military rifle. Note the slots milled into the bottom of the receiver for water drainage.

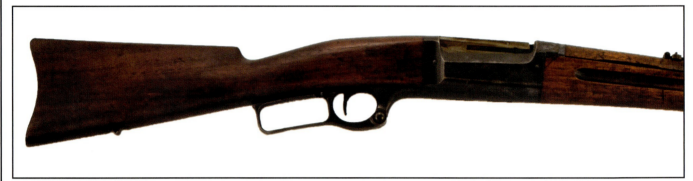

Figure 1-19. Pre-1899 military rifle. Note the bulge on the side of the receiver. This was probably necessary to handle a cartridge larger than the 303 Savage round.

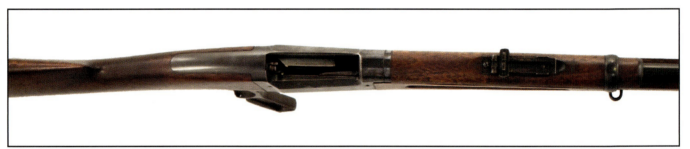

Figure 1-20. Pre-1899 military rifle. Note the longer tang and that the receiver is rather wide at the end of the loading/ejection opening (compare to Fig. 2-7).

Chapter 2

THE SAVAGE MODEL 1895

Introduction of the 1895, Savage's First Production Rifle

On April 5, 1894, Arthur Savage and a group of investors formed the Savage Repeating Arms Co. He had refined the design of the Model 1893 patent into a commercially viable rifle. Lacking the facilities to manufacture the firearm, they contracted with the Marlin Firearms Company of New Haven, Connecticut, to make the necessary tooling and equipment and produce the rifle. Opinions differ on how many 1895s were produced, but available data seems to indicate that serial numbers started at a little above 3000 and ended at 8000 plus for a total production of roughly 5,000 1895s (**see fig. 2-1 for a schematic of the redesigned action**).

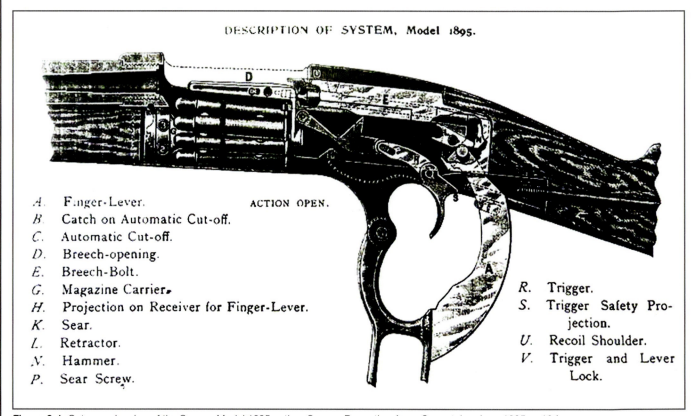

DESCRIPTION OF SYSTEM, Model 1895.

ACTION OPEN.

A. Finger-Lever.
B. Catch on Automatic Cut-off.
C. Automatic Cut-off.
D. Breech-opening.
E. Breech-Bolt.
G. Magazine Carrier.
H. Projection on Receiver for Finger-Lever.
K. Sear.
L. Retractor.
N. Hammer.
P. Sear Screw.

R. Trigger.
S. Trigger Safety Projection.
U. Recoil Shoulder.
V. Trigger and Lever Lock.

Figure 2-1. Cutaway drawing of the Savage Model 1895 action, Savage Repeating Arms Co. catalog June 1895, p 16.[1]

The Five Savage 1895 Models

The 1895 was cataloged with round, octagon, and half-octagon 26-inch barreled rifles; a carbine with a saddle ring, barrel band, and 22-inch barrel; and a full stocked military musket with a 30-inch barrel (**see figures 2-2 through 2-6**).

Figure 2-2. The author's Savage 1895 round barrel rifle, serial #7844.

Figure 2-3. Savage 1895 octagonal barrel rifle belonging to Ronald Coburn, retired CEO of Savage arms. Note the optional shotgun style stock and buttplate (serial #8111).

Figure 2-4. Savage 1895 half octagon barrel rifle belonging to Rick Ruetten. This rifle and the round barrel rifle in Fig. 2-2 have the standard crescent buttplate.

Figure 2-5. Savage 1895 carbine belonging to the J. Wright collection (serial #4616).

Figure 2-6. Savage 1895 military musket belonging to Doug Foglio (serial #5027).

Details of the 1895 carbine

The carbine came with a ladder-type rear sight, barrel band, and a carbine-type buttplate (**see figures 2-7, 2-8, and 2-9 for details on Doug Foglio's 1895 carbine, serial # 3358**).

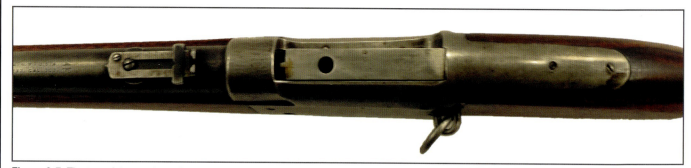

Figure 2-7. The top of the receiver of an 1895 carbine showing the opening for the cock/safe indicator on top of the bolt and the carbine-style ladder type rear sight.

Figure 2-8. The barrel band on an 1895 carbine.

Figure 2-9. The buttplate of an 1895 carbine. The musket had the same type of buttplate.

The 1895 musket has a provision for a socket bayonet like other military muskets of the era. Doug Foglio's musket looks the same as the musket pictured on page 15 in the 1897 catalog, which also shows an angular bayonet and a sword bayonet. These bayonets may not have been produced and were probably shown to solicit military orders. It is doubtful these bayonets could be attached to the few muskets that were produced (**see Fig. 2-10**).

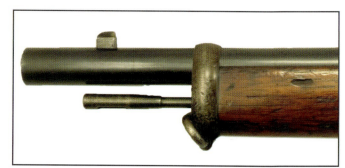

Figure 2-10. The muzzle of Doug Foglio's 1895 musket.

The 1895 musket featured a different ladder sight than the carbine (**see Fig. 2-11**).

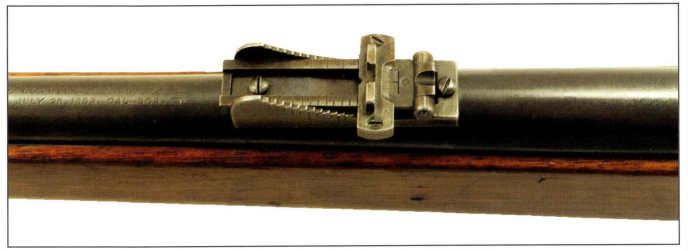

Figure 2-11. The rear ladder sight of Doug Foglio's 1895 musket (compare to the carbine sight in Fig. 2-7).

Characteristics of the Model 1895

The 1895 featured the rotary magazine from the earlier designs in a five-round capacity chambered for Arthur Savage's new smokeless powder 303 Savage ammunition. This round was similar in design to Winchester's 30-30, but was loaded with a heavier bullet. The 303 as loaded was slightly more powerful than the 30-30. The rifle featured a full loop lever and the bolt had a squared rear mating surface that came up and locked against the rear of the receiver when the lever was closed. See the 1893 prototype (**Fig. 1-13**) and the 1895 carbine (**Fig. 2-7**) for the square mating surface on the bolts. There is an opening in the top of the bolt that exposed the firing pin, which is engraved with a "C" for cocked and an "S" for safe (**see Fig. 2-7 for the 1895 cocking indicator and figure 3-4 for a comparison with the Model 1899 and 99 cocking indicators and bolt configurations**). There was another opening on the left side of the receiver that exposed the front of the rotary magazine, which was stamped with numbers one through five, allowing the shooter to see how many rounds were in the magazine. This was a carry-over from the Savage 1892 and 1893 prototypes (**see Figures 1-8, 1-14, and 2-12 for a comparison of the three round counters**).

Figures 2-12 and 2-13 show examples of the engraving available on the Model 1895s by Marlin's in-house engravers, John and Conrad Ulrich.

Figure 2-12. The counter that shows the number of rounds remaining in the magazine on an Ulrich engraved Model 1895 with a case hardened receiver. This photo and the one in Fig. 2-13 were taken by the author at the James D. Julia auction in March 2013.

Figure 2-13. The right side of an Ulrich engraved Savage Model 1895.

Figure 2-14. 1895 hard rubber buttplate.

The 1895 featured an internal hammer and a sliding safety on the right side of the lever, just behind the trigger, that blocks the trigger and locks the lever when pushed forward (**see Fig. 2-15**). The stock was secured by a bolt that ran longitudinally through the stock. This was much stronger and produced a potentially more accurate rifle than the industry standard tang bolts (**see the diagram in Fig. 2-1 and Fig. 4-8 for the stock through bolt**). The rifle was much sleeker in appearance than the other lever actions of the period. The 1895s were blued with a case-colored lever. A crescent buttplate was standard on the 26-inch barrel rifles, with a smooth steel shotgun type and a hard rubber buttplate optional. **Fig. 2-14** shows an 1895 hard rubber buttplate. Note it is marked SRAC for "Savage Repeating Arms Company"; the name was changed to Savage Arms Company in 1897. These hard rubber buttplates are usually found on rifles with other custom features. This particular 1895 has Circassian walnut stocks and a case-colored receiver.

A few of the rifles were made with a color case-hardened receiver (**see figures 2-12, 2-13, and 2-15**).

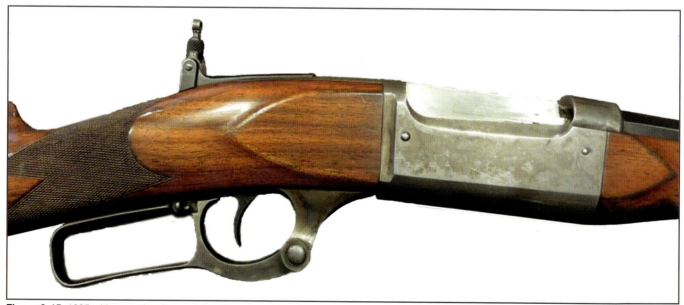

Figure 2-15. 1895 with an optional case colored receiver. Note the safety and lever lock just behind the trigger. The checkering and slimmed stock and forearm were probably not done at the factory.

Standard sights were the rocky mountain knife edge front sight and rocky mountain buckhorn rear sight (**see figures 2-16 and 2-17**).

The rifle's serial number was usually stamped on the buttstock under the buttplate (**see Fig. 2-18**). The 1899s and 99s produced until 1950 had the serial number stamped on the forearm, buttstock, and buttplate. The 1895 had the serial number stamped on the buttstock and buttplate.

The underside of the barrel is stamped with a "JM" or "M" to denote Marlin production. It is necessary to remove the forearm to see this stamp (**see Fig. 2-19**). The rifle pictured is the author's upgraded 1895 half octagon rifle and has both the "M" and "JM" stamps. This is the only 1895 I have seen with both markings, which may indicate it was sent back to Marlin for additional work.

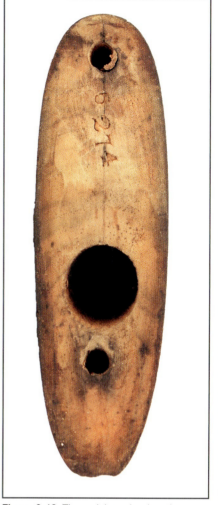

Figure 2-18. The serial number location on an 1895 stock.

Figure 2-16. Rocky mountain knife edge front sight.

Figure 2-17. Rocky mountain buckhorn rear sight.

Figure 2-19. The "JM" and "M" stamps used on Marlin-produced 1895s.

Ammunition for the New Rifle

Since the .303 cartridge was new, Arthur Savage had to find someone to produce ammunition for his rifle. Union Metallic Cartridge Co. filled this function until about 1900 (**see Fig. 2-20**). After that, Savage had to start producing their own ammunition, since the Ammunition Manufacturers Association— comprised of the Union Metallic Cartridge Co., Winchester Repeating Arms Co., and the U.S. cartridge Co.—refused to sell to Savage. Savage brand gunpowder may have been purchased from other sources, as the powder's blend varied during the early years. There is contradictory information on Savage ammo from about 1927 to 1935. Savage may have continued to produce their ammo until 1935 or USCC may have started producing the ammo in 1927. The Savage ammo had USCC primers during this period. However, Winchester had bought USCC at this time and continued making USCC stamped ammo. It is doubtful Winchester would have made ammo for Savage. There is also a possibility that Remington made the ammo

Figure 2-20. UMC ammo produced for the Savage 1895 in Rick Edmond's collection.

for Savage starting in 1927. Savage continued to market Savage brand ammo until 1963.

In 1897, the company changed its name to Savage Arms Company and was incorporated under West Virginia laws.

Savage's Attempt to Sell His Rifle to the New York National Guard

The various state militias started replacing their single-shot black powder rifles during the 1890s. The New York legislature passed a bill in 1895 to conduct trials for a new smokeless powder repeater for the New York National Guard. The weapons were required to have a magazine cutoff, safety trigger, and a cartridge counter. The savage was unanimously adopted by the commission. This rifle is probably the prototype shown in Figs. 1-16 through 1-20 on page 13 and 14. Several other manufacturers—Winchester in particular—claimed the commission was manipulated by Savage. Even

though no wrongdoing was proven, the selection was reversed by the governor and the state acquired obsolete Springfield single-shot 45–70 caliber black powder "trapdoor" rifles from the US government. At least one factor in this decision was the US government had a bill pending to give Springfields to the states. The contract with Savage for 15,000 rifles would have cost the state $300,000. The New York National Guard suffered heavily in combat during the Spanish-American war; their antiquated Springfields were no match against the Spanish, who were armed with Mausers that fired high-speed smokeless ammunition.[2]

1895 Barrel Address

Barrel addresses are shown at the end of chapters to make quick reference possible. They are also shown in Appendix A. Note the 1895 barrel address says "Savage Repeating

Arms Co." I have not seen any 1895s without the word "Repeating" in the barrel address.

Figure 2-21. Model 1895 barrel address on serial number 7428, belonging to Bill McNally.

Savage Reloading Tool

Savage contracted with the Ideal Manufacturing Company to produce a reloading tool for the .303 cartridge. This tool was available from the beginning of 1895 production and is shown in the June 1895 Savage Repeating Arms Co. catalog. The 100-grain bullets shown in the figure were produced to allow reloading light loads intended for gallery shooting.

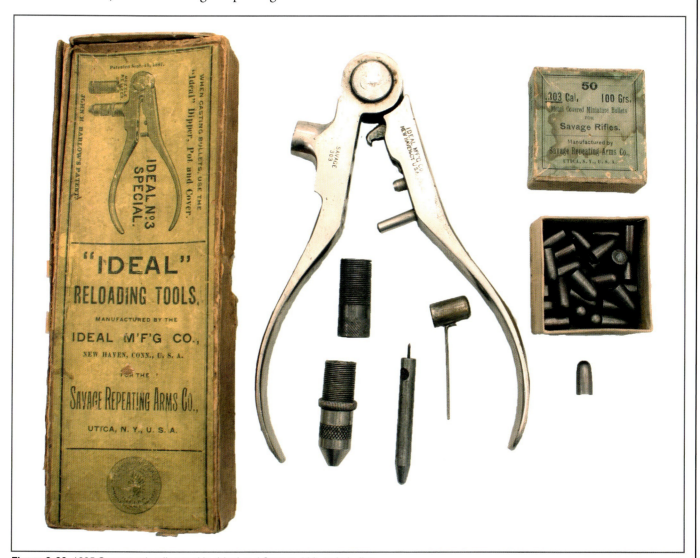

Figure 2-22. 1895 Savage reloading tool by Ideal and Savage 100-grain bullets.

Cody 1895 Military Musket

I have added photos of a variation of the 1895 musket that is in the Buffalo Bill Cody Museum's gun collection. It has a regular rifle stock like the ones used on the regular production 26-inch barrel Model 1895s. At least some of these muskets were returned to the factory and then sold to the public. This musket may have had the stock replaced by the factory due to damage to the original stock, or of course it could have been replaced by a subsequent owner. The stock is a correct 1895 stock (**see Fig. 2-23**). The Cody musket also has a rack number stamped on the receiver (**see Fig. 2-24**).

Figure 2-23. The Cody Firearms Museum's 1895 musket.

Figure 2-24. A closeup of the rack number on the Cody 1895 musket.

Chapter 3

THE INTRODUCTORY MODEL 1899^s

The Five Regular Production Models

By late 1898, the success of the 1895 had put Arthur Savage in a position to obtain financial backing to open a new production facility in Utica, New York. The rifle was redesigned and designated the Model 1899. Serial numbers started at 10.000. The new models were a 26-inch round barrel rifle, a 22-inch round barrel short rifle, a 26-inch octagon barrel rifle, a 26-inch half octagon barrel rifle, a 20-inch round barrel carbine with a saddle ring, and a 28-inch barrel military musket. The military musket was not regular production. **Fig. 3-1** shows the five regular production models.

Figure 3-1. The five regular production Model 1899s available starting in 1899: the top is 26-inch round barrel rifle serial #34.063; the second is 22-inch round barrel rifle serial #15.737 (later cataloged as the saddle rifle); third is 26-inch octagonal barrel rifle serial #180997; fourth is 26-inch half octagon barrel rifle serial #10.449; and fifth is 20-inch barrel carbine serial #192305 (see Fig. 3-5 for a comparison of 1899 and 1895 stocks and forearms).

The 1899 Military Musket

There may have been no more than two 1899 muskets produced. The early musket shown in **Fig. 3-2** belongs to Doug Foglio.

Fig. 3-3 shows the 1900 catalog photo of the military musket. It is the actual photo that appeared in the Model 1895 catalogs. Compare this photo with the rifle in **Fig. 3-2**. This photo is included here to show Savage's proposed bayonets to be included with the musket. These bayonets may have never been produced, but these images were probably included by the factory to encourage military orders.[1] For photos and information on a Savage Model 1899 military rifle produced for the Montreal Home Guard during World War I, see chapter 4.

Figure 3-2. Doug Foglio's 1899 military musket serial #53.504.

ANGULAR BAYONET.   SWORD BAYONET.

SAVAGE REPEATING HAMMERLESS MILITARY RIFLE.
Prices on application.

Length of Barrel,	28 inches.
Weight,	8¾ lbs.
Number of Cartridges,	6.
Caliber,	.303.

Figure 3-3. The military rifle from page 15 of the 1900 Savage Arms Catalog. This photo is a carry-over from the 1895 catalogs. Note the 1895 panels behind the receiver and the almost vertical comb on the buttstock.[1]

Characteristics of the Early Savage 1899

The new rifle featured a rectangular cocking indicator that protruded slightly above the top of the bolt when the rifle was cocked, allowing the shooter to feel as well as see when the rifle was cocked and eliminating the opening through the bolt into the firing pin channel. Eliminating the hole in the bolt reduced the possibility of debris or moisture getting into the channel. **Fig. 3-4** shows the four types of bolts and three types of cocking indicators.

Additionally the sear, firing pin, hammer, extractor, and retractor were redesigned and the stock and forearm were reshaped. For comparison of 1899 and 1895 forearms and stocks **see Fig. 3-5**.

Savage did use some leftover 1895 components on the earliest rifles. The half octagon barrel rifle serial number 10.449 (**Fig. 3-1**) has an 1895-type forearm numbered to the rifle.

Figure 3-4. The 1899 bolt continued to evolve during early production. The second from the top is the earliest 1899 bolt. The bolt face is similar to the 1895 (top). About 1904, the bolt face was redesigned to better enclose the base of the cartridge (third from top). In 1909, the cocking indicator was changed to a small round pin on the tang and the back of the bolt and the receiver mating surface were changed to a stronger, rounded shape (bottom). This cocking indicator and rounded rear bolt configuration remained unchanged until the end of 99 production.

Figure 3-5. Comparison of 1895 (top) and 1899 (bottom) forearms and buttstocks. The 1895 has a reverse curve in the bottom line of the forearm and a sharper vertical tip on the schnable. The 1895 has longer cheek panels that end in a smooth curve and a much steeper comb than the 1899.

The muzzles on all of the early rifles—except the carbine— were flat, with a slight bevel on the inner and outer surfaces. The carbine had a crowned muzzle (**see Fig. 3-6**). Savage offered a variety of sights on their rifles, some of which are shown here.

The 26-inch barrel rifles had crescent buttplates standard with a steel shotgun buttplate as a no cost option. The short rifle had a steel shotgun-type buttplate, although a few have been observed with a crescent buttplate. The carbine and musket had a military-type buttplate (**see Fig. 3-7**). The Savage "Screaming Indian" logo was added to the shotgun buttplate about 1904 (**see Fig. 3-8**).

For five dollars, the owner of an 1895 could send it back to the factory and have it converted to the new 1899 internals. The factory probably did not get a lot of takers on this offer. A new 1899 cost $20.00 to $21.50 at this time, making the five-dollar expenditure pretty steep for a minor alteration. I have hunted with an 1895 and have not had any problems with dirt or moisture getting into the firing pin channel, so I do not think there was much inducement to convert the 1895. The main advantage of the new cocking indicator would be for the shooter to feel whether the rifle was cocked or not.

Figure 3-8. The later corrugated shotgun type buttplate with the screaming Indian logo. This buttplate was used from about 1904 to 1928.

Figure 3-6. The different Model 1899 muzzles: at left is the carbine (caliber 38-55, serial #41.885; the other rifles are the ones shown in Fig. 3-1); second is the 22-inch round barrel; third is the 26-inch round barrel; and fourth is the octagonal barrel. The half octagon barrel muzzle is the same as the round barrel rifles.

Figure 3-7. The three types of standard buttplates: left is the carbine/musket buttplate, center is the short rifle shotgun-type buttplate, and right is the standard crescent buttplate used on the 26-inch barrel rifles.

Figure 3-9. A Savage leaf sight.

Figure 3-10. A Savage combination rear sight.

Standard sights were the rocky mountain knife edge front and rear buckhorn sights carried over from the model 1895 (**see Figures 2-16 and 2-17**). The rear sight with the screw and adjustable blade was changed to a non-adjustable variation within the first few years of production. Savage also offered a number of optional front, rear, and tang sights. A folding leaf rear sight was commonly used on the more expensive grades that usually came from the factory with a tang sight (**see Fig. 3-9**). Both leaves fold down so they do not obstruct the tang peep sight picture. See **Fig. 3-10** for a Savage combination tang sight on an engraved and checkered 1899 octagon barrel rifle.

With the beginning of 1899 production, Savage started stamping the rifle's serial number on the forearm, stock, and buttplate to facilitate final assembly. An unintentional added benefit is that it allows collectors to determine if these three components are original to the rifle (**see Fig. 3-11**). This practice was discontinued after 1950, when Savage started using production numbers unrelated to the serial number (**see chapter 6**).

Figure 3-11. Serial number 34063 stamped on the buttplate, buttstock, and rear of the forearm on an 1899 round barrel rifle.

Ammunition Available in the Early Savage 1899

Figure 3-12. Caliber .30 marking on an early 1899 30-30 Winchester rifle. Some 30-30s also had the Cal. .30 marking near the rear of the barrel and some had it in both places.

Figure 3-13. 25-35, 32-40, and 38-55 markings on early 1899 rifles.

The rifles were only available in 303 Savage caliber in 1899; 30-30 Winchester was added in 1900 and 25-35, 32-40, and 38-55 Winchester were added in 1903. The early 30-30s were marked "caliber 30" (**see Fig. 3-12**). The other Winchester caliber rifles were marked 25-35, etc., without the Winchester name (**see Fig. 3-13**).

All five regular-production models were available in all five calibers. The 1903 catalog stated the musket was available in .303 or 30-30. The musket was no longer cataloged by 1905. Production in calibers 25-35, 32-40, and 38-55 was fairly low and they were dropped in 1917. This was probably due to low demand, as these cartridges were not as powerful as the .303 and 30-30. Since fewer Savage 1899s were produced in these three calibers they bring a premium price in today's market. The 30-30 caliber was discontinued about 1941.

Serial Number Characteristics

Starting with serial number 10.000, the serial number had a dot (period) between the second and third digit. I use this dot while referring to these serial numbers in this book. At some point between 90.000 and 100000 the dot was dropped (**see Fig. 3-14**).

Figure 3-14. The top rifle has the five-digit serial number with the dot between digits two and three and below is a later five-digit number without the dot. The numbers have been enhanced with white to make them more readable. These rifles are in the Don Johnson collection.

Model 1899 Designations Used in Common Practice

In common practice the 1899s are designated as follows:

- 26-inch round barrel rifle - Model 1899A
- 22-inch round barrel rifle - Model 1899A short rifle
- 26-inch octagon barrel rifle - Model 1899B
- 26-inch half octagon barrel rifle - Model 1899C
- 28-inch military musket - Model 1899D
- 20-inch Carbine - Model 1899F, also commonly called the saddle ring carbine

The letter designations did not appear in Savage's catalogs until 1920; until then, the rifles were identified by 26-inch round barrel, 20-inch carbine, etc. The above designations came from the telegraphic codes used to order the rifles (**see Fig. 3-15**). For simplicity I will use the letter designations 1899A, 1899B, etc.

A number of extras were available, including pistol grips, cheek pieces, higher grades of walnut, checkering, engraving, and plating on all models and longer barrels on Models 1899A, B, and C (**see Figure 3-16**).

Some examples of 1899 engraving are covered below. The Model 99 engraved rifles are in chapters 5, 7, and 8. My next book will go in depth on the subject of engraving and other special features offered on the Savage lever action rifles.

Telegraphic and Cable Code.

Cable Address:—" SAVAGE, UTICA."

SPORTING RIFLES.

	ROUND.	OCT.	HALF OCT.
.303 cal., 26-inch barrel,	Abate.	Bait.	Cub.
.303 cal., 26-inch barrel, shotgun butt plate,	Abit.	Bill.	Can.
.303 cal., 22-inch barrel, shotgun butt plate,	Aback.	——	——
.303 cal., 28 inch barrel,	Abed.	Bale.	Cat.
.303 cal., 30-inch barrel,	Abode.	Barb.	Cake.

MILITARY RIFLES.

.303 cal., 28-inch barrel,	Dace.

CARBINES.

.303 cal., 20-inch barrel,	Fig.

CARTRIDGES.

.303 cal. Savage Smokeless Powder Cartridges,	Kail.
.303 cal. Savage Smokeless Powder Expanding Bullet Cartridges,	Kedge.
.303 cal. Savage Smokeless Powder Miniature Bullet Cartridges,	Keep.
.303 cal. Savage Paper-patched Bullet Cartridges,	Kin.
.303 cal. Savage Smokeless Powder Miniature Metal-Covered Bullet Cartridges,	Kiss.
.30 cal. U. S. Government Smokeless Powder Cartridges,	Kernel.

SHELLS.

.303 cal. Savage Regular Shells,	Label.
.303 cal. Savage Miniature Shells,	Lace.
.30 cal. U. S. Government Shells,	Lackey.

Figure 3-15. Page 54 of the Savage Arms Co. 1900 catalog showing telegraphic codes used to order rifles and ammunition.[2]

Savage Rifle.

EXTRAS.

Barrels can not be supplied longer than 30 inches.	
Additional length over standard per inch,	$ 1.00
Fancy American Walnut Stock and Fore-arm,	5.00
Fancy English Walnut Stock and Fore-arm,	10.00
Fancy Circassian Walnut Stock and Fore-arm,	15.00
Checking Butt Stock and Fore-arm (Style as shown on page 4),	5.00
Checking Butt Stock and Fore-arm (Style as shown on page 6),	8.00
Nickel-plated Trimmings,	2.50
Full Nickel Plating, except barrel,	4.00
Silver-plated Trimmings,	4.00
Full Silver Plating, except barrel,	$10.00
Gold-plated Trimmings,	10.00
Full Gold Plating, except barrel,	22.00
Matted Barrels,	5.00
Extra finish on ordinary stock,	2.00
Swivel and sling strap,	1.00
Leaving off rear sight slot,	1.00
Changing position rear sight slot,	1.00
Cheek Piece,	6.00
Pistol Grip,	5.00
Altering length of butt stock or drop (See page 27),	10.00

ENGRAVING.

Grade A. Page 3,	$ 5.00
Grade B. " 4,	10.00
Grade C. " 5,	20.00
Grade D. " 6,	30.00
Grade E. Page 7,	$ 40.00
Grade F. " 8,	50.00
Grade G. " 9, and as shown on back cover,	130.00
Name and Scroll,	2.00

SUNDRIES.

Canvas Covers,	$ .75
Canvas Covers, leather bound,	1.90
Pliable Leather Cover,	3.00
Solid Leather Case,	5.00
Carbine Holster,	2.00
Cartridge Belt,	1.00
Brass Cleaning Rod,	.30
Brass Cleaning Rod, with revolving handle,	$ .50
Brass Cleaning Rod, revolving handle, jointed,	.50
Brass Wire Cleaning Brush,	.25
Hickory Cleaning Rod,	.10
Field Cleaner,	.50
"Three in One," per bottle (See page 28),	.25
.303 Savage Gun Grease, per tube (See page 28),	.15

Figure 3-16. Page 26 of the Savage Arms 1900 Catalog showing extras, engraving, and sundries.[3]

A Brief Coverage of Engraving Available for Savage 1899s

Enoch Tue was Savage's in-house engraver. He was trained at Churchill's in England and produced some exquisite engraving. Some examples of his engraving are shown in the following figures, from the least expensive to the most expensive (**see Figures 3-17 through 3-29**). Unless stated otherwise, these rifles were photographed at the James D. Julia auction in March 2013 by the author.

Figure 3-17. Grade A engraving. The right side is essentially the same and not shown.

Figure 3-18. The left side of Grade B engraving. The receiver of this rifle has been stippled—an enhancement that appeared on a number of Enoch Tue's engraved rifles. This rifle letters as having been sold to Enoch Tue. There is a squirrel engraved on the bottom of the receiver. "B" engraving does not usually have engraving on the bottom of the receiver, so Mr. Tue probably enhanced his personal rifle.

Figure 3-19. Right side of the Grade B engraving on Enoch Tue's rifle.

Figure 3-20. Left side of the Grade C engraving on Dick Johnson's 1899H.

Figure 3-21. Right side of the Grade C engraving on Dick Johnson's 1899H.

Figure 3-22. The left side of Grade D engraving. This rifle belongs to Dick Johnson.

Figure 3-23. The right side of Grade D engraving.

Figure 3-24. The left side of Grade E engraving.

Figure 3-25. The right side of Grade E engraving.

Figure 3-26. The right side of Grade F engraving. *Courtesy James D. Julia Auctions, Fairfield, Maine*

Figure 3-27. The left side of Grade F engraving.

Figure 3-28. The right side of the G engraving.

Figure 3-29. The left side of the Grade G engraving.

Figure 3-30. Grade A2 engraving. Both sides are essentially the same. *Courtesy of James D. Julia Auctions, Fairfield, Maine*

Figure 3-31. The left side of Monarch Grade engraving. This was the highest grade of standard engraving done by Enoch Tue.

Figure 3-32. The right side of Monarch Grade engraving. *Courtesy of James D. Julia Auctions, Fairfield, Maine*

By 1905, Savage started offering various types of engraving in packages with special wood and checkering or carving. At this time Grade A2 engraving was introduced, which was a less intricate grade of engraving than grade A (**see Figure 3-30**).

- The former Grade A engraving was offered in two models: Grade AB, which had dark curly American walnut stocks; and Grade BC, which was the same as AB, except for plain American walnut stocks. Both had pistol grips and checkering.
- Leader grade had the former Grade B engraving coupled with fancy figured American walnut and fancier checkering than Grades AB and BC.
- Crescent Grade had the Grade C engraving and grade C checkering, which was a higher grade checkering than the Leader grade.
- Victor grade had the former Grade D engraving, fancy English walnut, and the same checkering as the Crescent grade rifle.

- Rival Grade had the former Grade E engraving with Circassian walnut and the same checkering as the Crescent grade, as well as the owner's name engraved on the bottom of the receiver.
- Premier Grade has the Grade F engraving with fancy checkering and Circassian walnut and the owner's name engraved on the bottom of the receiver.
- Monarch Grade had a new engraving style coupled with hand-carved "specially imported wood"[4] and a hand-finished inside mechanism (**see Figures 3-31 and 3-32**).

The grades of engraving sometimes showed up under other designations in different catalogs; the names also changed occasionally. For example, a Rival grade rifle might have F engraving. In reality, the grades above Leader Grade showed a great deal of variation and were probably created at the whim of the person ordering the rifle or Savage factory personnel. Engraving, checkering, carved stocks, and other special features will be addressed in my next book.

Barrel Addresses for 1899 to 1904

Barrel addresses changed several times during 1899 production (**see Figures 3-33 and 3-34 for barrel addresses used on early 1899s**). Note that the 1899 to 1904 barrel address is similar to the 1895 barrel address, except it says "Savage Arms Co" and not "Savage Repeating Arms Co," as is the case on the 1895 (**for the later 1899 barrel addresses see Figures 4-31 and 4-32 at the end of Chapter 4**). There are at least two variations of this. The one shown in Fig. 3-33 is very early and has dots between the curlies and the company identification. Another variation does not have the dots, making the top line shorter than the bottom, and another does not have the dots, but does have the "Oct. 3, '99." patent date, as well as the two earlier patent dates.

Figure 3-33. The early 1899 barrel address used until about 1904.

Figure 3-34. The Savage 1899 barrel address 1904–1911.

Chapter 4

MODELS INTRODUCED FROM 1904 TO 1915

Including the Montreal Home Guard Musket and Changes Made through 1920

Savage announced in their 1903 catalog that they had greatly expanded the factory and their intention was to add different types of arms as fast as possible.[1] They did add a number of non-1899 arms, but they also expanded the 1899 line over the next few years.

The First New Model 1899, the 1899H

In 1905, Savage introduced a radical new featherweight Model 1899 rifle (**see Figure 4-1**). It featured a rapidly tapered 20-inch barrel with a crowned muzzle. The 1899H also featured a shotgun-style stock with a hard rubber buttplate or an optional metal buttplate. It had a shorter, thinner forearm than the other models (**See Fig. 4-2 for a comparison between the barrel and forearm of an 1899H and an 1899F [SRC]**). These two rifles have the same barrel length and are the same overall length, but the carbine is advertised as weighing seven and one-quarter pounds, compared to the featherweight's six pounds. All of the stocks and some forearms were drilled out to reduce weight (**see Fig. 4-3**). The front sight base was brazed to the barrel and the sight blade was held to the base with a small screw. The

early front sights were close to the muzzle, while the later ones were moved back to the same front sight location as the other 1899s (**see Figure 4-4**). The standard rear sight was a Savage Micrometer that was both windage and elevation adjustable. The 1899H was initially available in calibers 25-35, 30-30, and .303. Savage catalogs stated that checkering and engraving were available for the featherweight, but that fancy wood was not available. The rifle in **Fig. 4-1** is a matching number rifle with fancy wood. I have also observed several other 1899Hs that had fancy wood. The 1899H was eventually offered in takedown and the Savage 22 Hi-Power cartridge and will be addressed further.

Figure 4-1. The Savage Model 1899H Featherweight introduced in 1905. This rifle (serial number 79728) was produced in 1908.

Figure 4-2. Comparison of the featherweight with a standard barrel rifle: the rifle at the top is an 1899H Featherweight and the bottom rifle is an 1899F carbine. The carbine is equipped with a windage adjustable rear sight similar to the standard Featherweight rear sight. This Featherweight is equipped with a folding leaf rear sight frequently found on rifles equipped with a tang sight.

Figure 4-3. The hard rubber buttplate and hollowed out buttstock and forearm used on the 1899H Featherweight in Fig. 4-1.

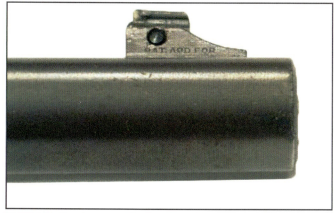

Figure 4-4. The front sight base is brazed to the barrel. This rifle has an optional white ivory bead sight pinned to the base. The factory attached all the front sights with a screw and did not pin the front sights on the 1899H. This sight must have been attached aftermarket.

The Lightweight Perris Special

In 1904, concurrent with the development of the Featherweight, Savage was also working on a special-order rifle called the "Perris Special" that was designed by A. E. Perris of San Bernardino, California. It appears as though the only difference between the Perris rifle and the Featherweight was the Perris had a straight tapered barrel. Mr. Perris's specifications are not available, but it appears he wanted a sharper tapered 20-inch barrel that was smaller at the muzzle than the 1899F saddle ring carbine's barrel and therefore a little lighter. Savage argued against this, as it would require new barrel-making machinery and a hand-fitted forearm at greatly added cost. There is some controversy as to whether Savage copied Perris's idea but with the convex tapered barrel, or if they had the Featherweight under development before Perris contacted them with his proposal. Unfortunately, some of the correspondence regarding this matter is unavailable. After the Featherweight was introduced A. E. Perris questioned why Savage went ahead with his project while a similar rifle was being developed by the factory. Savage's response was that they did not want to release details of the new rifle until it was available to the public.

Mr. Perris was hoping his rifle would become regular production, but Savage said it was not cost effective to produce two similar rifles.

It appears as though at least thirty rifles were produced according to Mr. Perris's specifications and engraved "Perris Specials" on the left side of the receiver.[2]

The Savage Model 1899CD

Figure 4-5. Octagonal barrel 1899CD serial number 53.258, .303 caliber.

Figure 4-6. Round barrel takedown 1899CD serial number 130022, .303 caliber.

The 1905 catalog also shows eight special rifles that have different grades of engraving, checkering, and wood.[3] Douglas Murray treats one of these (the 1899CD) as a separate model.[4] This is kind of a fuzzy area. It could simply be a set of options available on the other basic rifles and has no different status than the other seven Special rifles listed on pages twenty-nine to thirty-two of Catalog No. 15 and subsequent catalogs. The 1899CD options were a pistol grip and checkering. A number of very knowledgeable people contend the 1899CD is a separate model. For that reason I am including photos of two 1899CDs that according to John Callahan, Savage Historian, are 1899CDs. **Fig. 4-5** is an early 1899CD with an octagon barrel and **Fig. 4-6** a later 1899CD with a round takedown barrel. Note the earlier rifle has a straight lever identical to the straight stocked rifles and the latter has a slightly curved lever. Savage started producing the curved lever for pistol grip rifles about 1906. Both rifles are in the John Wright collection. These features were available on the featherweight solid frame and takedown rifles when they became available. They were also designated 1899CDs as shown in Savage's ledgers.

Perch belly buttstocks

About 1908 or 1909, Savage started putting a distinct curve on the lower line of the buttstock called a perch belly; it was continued until about 1917 (**see Fig. 4-5 for a straight line buttstock and 4-6 and 4-6a for a perch belly buttstock**). The degree of curve varied somewhat, probably due to the hand work involved producing the stocks.

Figure 4-6a. A perch belly buttstock compared to an earlier straight stock.

A Few Notes About Early Catalogs

As late as Catalog No. 15, many of the rifles shown have 1895 stocks and fore ends. Savage was still using photos of Model 1895s in their catalogs as late as 1905. By Catalog No. 17 (about 1906), the rifles shown had 1899-type stocks and fore ends.

The covers of Savage catalogs got pretty colorful by 1903. By 1905, they were putting out multiple catalogs per year and usually numbering them instead of dating them. Catalog No. 17 is a small version that does not have as much information as the larger-format catalogs. The cover of No. 17 is shown in **Fig. 4-7**.

Figure 4-7. Cover of Savage Arms Co. Catalog No. 17, probably 1906.

Introduction of the Savage 1899 Takedown Rifle

Up until about 1906, Savage said it was not possible to make a reliable takedown rifle. They advocated taking the stock off so the rifle would fit into a piece of luggage, but there were several drawbacks to this. Even with the lever open, a 26-inch barrel rifle was thirty-three inches long. If the lever was closed the rifle was about thirty-six inches long. It also required having a heavy-bladed screwdriver to reattach the stock bolt and a smaller one to reattach the buttplate once the destination was reached. This also took quite a bit more time than reassembling a true takedown (**see Fig. 4-8**).

Figure 4-8. An 1899A with the stock removed and the tools necessary to reattach the stock.

Figure 4-9. The release for a prototype Savage 1899 takedown.

The Savage factory has an early prototype takedown with a top release that looks a lot like an aftermarket tang safety (**see Fig. 4-9**). The rear of the barrel has what appears to be a sleeve over it (**see Fig. 4-10**). Unfortunately, we were not able to take this rifle out of the case to make further examination of how it worked.

By 1907, Savage was producing an 1899 with a workable takedown feature for the 22- and 26-inch round barrel rifles (**see Fig. 4-11 for a photo of an 1899A takedown**). Some of these takedowns had the last three digits of the rifle's serial number stamped on the bottom of the barrel.

With the action open, the forearm is removed and a square slot in the forearm is fitted onto the forearm lug on the bottom of the barrel. The barrel could then be unscrewed from the receiver (**see Fig. 4-11a**).

The barrel and receiver have interrupted threads; it only requires a quarter turn counterclockwise to remove the barrel. When the rifle is reassembled, the barrel and receiver are securely locked together by the raised steel tab on the rear of the forearm that engages the slots on the barrel and receiver (**see Fig. 4-12**).

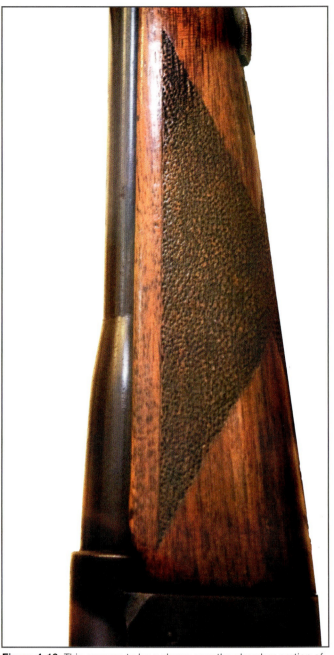

Figure 4-10. This appears to be a sleeve over the chamber portion of the barrel of the prototype 1899 takedown.

Figure 4-11. Darrel Russel's 1899A takedown, serial #106756, caliber 30-30.

Figure 4-11a. 1899A takedown with the forearm removed.

Figure 4-12. 1899 takedown with the barrel removed. The metal lug on the collar on the rear of the forearm engages the slots on the barrel and receiver, locking the barrel firmly to the receiver.

Introduction of the Takedown Feature in the 1899H

In 1909, Catalog No. 24 announced the addition of an 1899H Featherweight with the takedown feature (**see Fig. 4-13**).

The catalog also offered extra barrels for the lightweight takedown at $10.00 each.[5] Since calibers 32-40 and 38-55 were never offered in either version of the 1899H, the takedown barrel options were limited to 25-35, 303, 30-30, and 22 H-P (not available until 1912). At this point, all the round-barrel rifles except the 1899F saddle ring carbine were offered in takedown. The takedown feature was never a standard option for the carbine, octagon, and half octagon rifles.

Figure 4-13. The Savage 1899H .22 Hi-Power Featherweight takedown (serial #123958) produced in 1912.

Change in the Cartridge Counter View Hole

With the changeover in 1909 to the rounded rear bolt/receiver mating surface mentioned in Chapter 3 and shown in **Fig. 3-4**, the cartridge counter viewing hole was changed to an oval (**see Fig. 4-14**). This configuration was continued until about 1985 on most models. Chapter 7 has more details about rifles without the counter.

Figure 4-14. The lower rifle has the round viewing hole used until about serial number 90.000. The upper rifle has the later oval viewing hole.

Introduction of the 22 Savage Hi-Power Cartridge

In 1912, Savage offered a new cartridge, the Savage 22 Hi-Power. Charles Newton, who was well known for developing wildcat cartridges, necked down a 25-35 Winchester to create the new cartridge for Savage. The .228-inch diameter 70-grain pointed bullet was advertised as having a muzzle velocity of 2,800 feet per second, which exceeded the muzzle velocity of the 30-06 cartridges available at the time (**see Fig. 4-16**) for a round nose version. The cartridge was only offered in the lightweight takedown 1899H (**shown in Fig. 4-13**) at this time.[6] The Savage's magazine allowed the use of pointed bullets, but the tubular magazines of its competitors did not, since the point of a bullet would be resting on the primer of the one in front of it. This could result in the point of a bullet detonating the bullet ahead with disastrous results for the rifle, shooter, and anyone nearby.

Figure 4-15. Savage advertisement showing a dead tiger taken with a .22 Hi-Power.[7]

Savage called the rifle the "Imp," and over the next few years made some pretty wild claims about the cartridge's capabilities. They even ran an advertisement showing a tiger killed with a 22 High Power (**see Fig. 4-15**).

Wyoming supposedly limited the taking of elk and larger game to ammunition of .243-inch or larger diameter due to the number of animals wounded and lost with the 22 H-P. This ruling is still in effect at the time of this writing in 2015. Some old-timers have verified that it was not effective on larger animals, but was popular with sheep herders for use on coyotes. I made a clean kill on a pronghorn with a Savage 22 Hi-Power at 240 yards. The bullet broke the pronghorns back. Shot placement is very important to make clean kills.

Introduction of the 250-3000 Savage Cartridge

Figure 4-17. Savage 1899 250-3000 rifle with its shipping box and end label. The top of the box is plain with the serial number hand-written on it. From the Bill McNally collection (serial #184567).

In 1914, Charles Newton shortened and necked down the 30-06 cartridge to a new .257-inch diameter cartridge for Savage called the 250-3000 Savage. The 3000 part of the nomenclature designated the fact that the 87-grain bullet had a muzzle velocity of over 3,000 feet per second (**see Fig. 4-16**).

Charles Newton requested that Savage load the round with a 100-grain bullet that was more effective on deer-size game. This gave a 2,800fps velocity with the powders available at the time. Savage refused to do this at first because they wanted to maintain the glamor of the 3,000fps claim that could only be obtained by the 87-grain bullet. This was the fastest commercial cartridge available at the time and the only one that exceeded 3,000 fps. Savage and other manufacturers eventually loaded the round with 100-grain bullets. It is

Figure 4-16. Left is the .22 Hi-Power and right, the 250-3000 Savage cartridges.

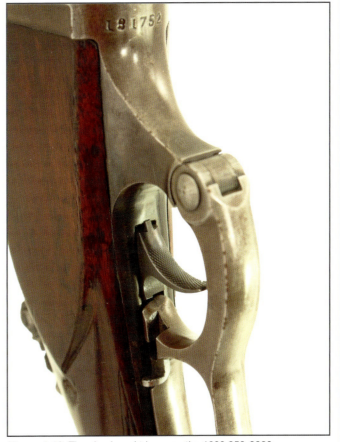

Figure 4-18. The checkered trigger on the 1899 250-3000.

now possible to load the 100-grain bullet to 3,000+ fps with modern gun powder. The early 250-3000's barrel twist rate was 1 in 14 inches which doesn't stabilize 100 grain or heavier bullets very well resulting in poor accuracy. The 250-3000's produced after 1960 had a 1 in 10 twist rate and are accurate with 100 grain bullets.

Savage also offered this cartridge exclusively in an all new rifle designated Model 1899 250-3000. The standard

features on this rifle were a 22-inch featherweight takedown barrel, a rather fat perchbelly stock with a capped pistol grip, hand-checkered forearm and pistol grip, and a checkered trigger. The pre–World War I 1899 250-3000 was the only 99 ever offered with a checkered trigger (**see Figures 4-17 and 4-18**). Savage started phasing in serrated triggers around this time frame (1917–1918) on all models.

The Montreal Home Guard Musket

Canada joined England when England entered World War I on the side of the Allies in August 1914. Canada's small regular military and National Guard were sent to Europe almost immediately, creating a need for troops to guard bridges and public buildings. Men under forty were recruited quickly to go to Europe, pretty much leaving men over forty the task of guarding Canada. There was a general fear in Canada that the Germans were going to invade the country. There was no shortage of volunteers and home guards were formed quickly in a number of jurisdictions. One of the problems was arming the new home guard. All military firearms, including the Canadian-built Ross rifle, were

needed in Europe. Prominent citizens of Montreal, Quebec, started forming a home guard in the fall of 1914 and by mid-January 1915 had established a permanent structure. It was determined in late 1914 that a standardized rifle was needed. The guard's maximum requirement of 2,500 rifles was considered too small for consideration by the regular manufacturers of military firearms. The MHG then turned to the Savage Arms Co. Savage agreed to manufacture a rifle of musket configuration that could accommodate a bayonet (**see Fig. 4-19**). Included in the deal was the rifle, a bayonet of Savage manufacture, and a sling. The rifle had the same 26-inch round barrel, barrel address, and high-

Figure 4-19. Savage Montreal Home Guard Musket with a standard 26-inch barrel (serial #168363). The earlier 1899 musket had a 28-inch barrel.

Figure 4-20. MHG hand guard and rear ladder sight. The pre-WWI 1899 musket did not have a hand guard. For photos of the earlier musket see Figures 3-2 and 3-3.

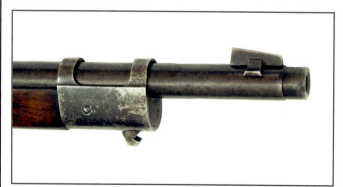

Figure 4-21. MHG bayonet lug and muzzle turned down to accommodate the bayonet.

Figure 4-22. Savage stamped this number on the buttplate for record keeping purposes.

gloss blue receiver as Savage's regular production 1899s. It had a musket-type full-length forearm, hand guard, and a rear ladder sight (**see Fig. 4-20**). It had a bayonet lug and the muzzle was turned down to accommodate the bayonet (**see Fig. 4-21**). It also had a military buttstock and buttplate the same as the Savage 1899F SRC (**see Fig. 4-22**). The Canadians wanted it produced in the .303 Enfield caliber, but that would have increased development costs and, most importantly, increased the time to start deliveries, so the Canadians settled for the Savage 303 caliber. [8] The muskets were produced in 1914 and 1915 in the serial number range 162,000 to 175,500.[9] The first shipment was early December 1914, with serial numbers in the range 164XXX, then three shipments on three consecutive days in late December 1914 with serial numbers in the 165XXX range. Serial numbers in the 168XXX range shipped in February 1915 and serial numbers in the 173XXX range in April 1915. The hand guard covered the caliber marking on the early rifles. Rifles after about serial number 1654XX had the caliber stamped on the receiver ring. The MHG supplied rack numbers to Savage that were applied to the top of the buttplate at the factory. The highest known number stamped on the buttplate of one of these rifles is 1015 (**see Fig. 4-22 for the location of this number**).[10] A few muskets have been observed without rack numbers and would have been shipped to someone other than the MHG. Guard members were allowed to bring their own rifles and rifles other than Savage Model 1899Ds have been identified with rack numbers in the same range as the Savages, indicating probably less than 1,000 Savage muskets were produced.

The guardsmen who bought their own muskets had the option of having their name inscribed on the left side of the receiver. This may have been done at Savage, but was probably done after the guardsman received his rifle in Montreal (**see Fig. 4-23**).

Many of the muskets were purchased by companies who recruited their employees to serve in the guard. These company-owned muskets were not inscribed on the receiver, but many had the employee's name stamped on the buttstock (**see Fig. 4-23a**).

The guardsmen's uniforms included a unique hat badge (**see Figure 4-24**).

Figure 4-23a. Guardsman's name and record keeping number stamped on top of the buttstock on Steve Ballek's musket (serial #165305).

Figure 4-23. Inscribed MHG musket. The musket was produced in 1915. The 1914 date indicates that John D. Baile joined the MHG in 1914.

Figure 4-24. Hat badge worn by members of the Montreal Home Guard.

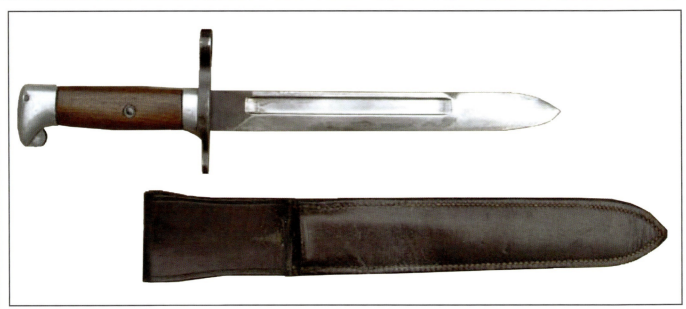

Figure 4-25. The Savage MHG bayonet with scabbard. *This photo and Figures 4-26 to 4-28 courtesy of Blair Power*

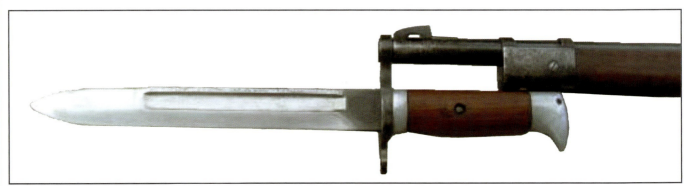

Figure 4-26. The Savage MHG bayonet mounted on a Savage 1899 MHG musket.

Figure 4-27. The Savage logo on an MHG bayonet.

Figure 4-28. MHG guardsmen with their Savage 1899 muskets.

Savage also produced a special bayonet for the MHG musket that had a unique attachment mechanism and the Savage screaming Indian logo (**see Figures 4-25 through 4-27**). There are very few of these bayonets in existence and they bring a high price on the collector's market.

The photo in **Fig. 4-28** shows some MHG guardsmen with their 1899 Savage muskets.

The Montreal Home Guard did engage would-be saboteurs on a number of occasions and are credited with saving several bridges.[10]

As is common with military rifles, many of the MHG muskets were sproterized after the war, adding to the difficulty of finding an intact Savage MHG musket.

Savage Arms' Involvement in World War I

Figure 4-29. World War I Lewis machine gun produced by Savage Arms Co. J. Wright collection.

The Driggs-Seabury Ordnance Company bought Savage in 1915 with the intent of getting into production of war materiel for Europe. The company went by the name Driggs-Seabury for a time, but no 1899s were marked Driggs-Seabury. They changed the name to Savage Arms Corporation a year or two later. The new corporation produced Lewis machine guns and other ordnance during World War I (**see Fig. 4-29 for a photo of a Lewis machine gun produced by Savage**).

Figure 4-30. Label from the transit box produced by Savage for their Lewis machine guns. J. Wright collection.

I am including a photo of the label from the Savage-produced transit box for the Lewis gun simply because a piece of military equipment does not normally have such a colorful label (**see Figure 4-30**).

Production capability was greatly expanded during the war. The octagon and half-octagon barrel rifles were probably dropped about 1916, as Savage started changing over to war materiel production. It is generally believed that the 1899B and 1899C were dropped in 1915, but the author has an 1899B produced in 1916. Production of 1899s was low in 1917 and few if any were produced during 1918.

With the war over and Savage's increased production facilities available for civilian goods they jumped back into

the market, with almost 20,000 1899s produced in 1919. The 1899 250-3000 was redesigned with a non-perchbelly buttstock, with the bottom of the stock forming a straight line from the pistol grip back. It shared a serrated trigger with the other Model 1899s. The smooth trigger was replaced on the other models about this time. The 1899F saddle ring carbine was discontinued about 1919. The author has an 1899F (serial number 192305) that letters as shipped in 1919. The serial number falls into the 1917 serial number range, but it was not assembled and shipped until 1919. Rick Edmonds has seen SRCs with serial numbers up to 202,300.

Barrel Addresses for 1905 to 1926

Barrel address markings between 1905 and 1911 are shown in **Fig. 3-34** in Chapter 3. The barrel address for 1911 to 1919 is shown in **Fig. 4-31** and 1919 to 1926 in **Fig. 4-32**.

Figure 4-31. Barrel address used on Savage 1899s from about 1911 to 1919.

Figure 4-32. Savage 1899 barrel address 1919–1926.

Chapter 5

CONTINUATION OF THE OLD MODELS UNDER NEW NAMES

New Models Introduced from 1920 to 1927, and Changes Before 1932

Introduction of the 300 Savage Cartridge

Savage started off the new decade by introducing another revolutionary cartridge. Savage engineers created the new cartridge (300 Savage) by shortening the 30-06 government cartridge to fit the Savage action. To get the maximum amount of powder in the case it was full diameter as far forward as possible with a sharp shoulder and short neck (**see Fig. 1**). Savage claimed it equaled the 30-06 in performance with a 150-grain bullet at a muzzle velocity of 2,700 feet per second. This statement was fairly accurate with the gun powders available at the time, although they may have been comparing muzzle velocities between the 150-grain 300 and a heavier 30-06 bullet. The 300 was Savage's primary cartridge until the late 1950s, and was available in at least some models most of the time until the end of production. Production of the 300 dropped off sharply after Savage started offering the 308 in the Model 99s. The cartridge is still an effective game getter, with a number of people, including the author, using it to hunt big game (**see Fig. 5-2**).

Figure 5-1. Early 150-grain 300 Savage Arms Corporation metal jacket bullet.

Figure 5-2. The author with a caribou killed with a 1950 vintage Savage Model 99R in caliber 300 Savage.

The Change from the Savage Model 1899 to Model 99

Savage started using letter designations for the various Model 1899s about 1920. There is some controversy about whether these earliest rifles were designated 1899A, B, C, etc., or if they started out as 99A, B, C, etc. A few historian letters have turned up using the 1899B designation for round barrel takedowns produced in 1920 and some Savage literature also uses this designation, including catalog #62 (c. 1920); this may be another discrepancy in the catalogs. Savage historian John T. Callahan has assured me that Savage didn't officially drop the "18" until about 1923. A

point of confusion is that we use letter designations for the pre-WWI rifles; for example, the pre-WWI 1899B was the octagon barrel rifle that was discontinued about 1916. If the 26-inch round barrel takedown rifle was then designated 1899B this would cause some confusion, as they are entirely different rifles. Savage didn't have this problem because they didn't use the letter designations until after WWI. These designations are a more recent invention thought by collectors to simplify the terminology for the early rifles.

The Savage Models 99A, 99B, 99C, and 99D

Figure 5-3. Savage Models 99B (top), 99C (middle), and 99D (bottom). The 99A was unchanged from the earlier Model 1899A (see the top rifle in Fig. 3-1) and had the same features as the 99B, except it was solid frame. The 99B pictured is in 30-30 caliber and the C and D are in .300 Savage with 24-inch barrels.

About 1923, the standard weight round 26-inch-barrel solid frame became the 99A (1899A) and the 26-inch barrel takedown became the 99B (1899B). For the purpose of this book I will use the designations without the "18" prefix for the 1923 and later rifles (**see Table 5-1**). The crescent buttplate was continued on these two models. The standard weight short barrel rifles were replaced by the 99C (1899C) solid frame and the 99D (1899D) takedown rifles. The 99Cs

and 99Ds featured a shotgun-type butt with a steel buttplate and 22-inch barrels in 303 Savage and 30-30 Winchester and 24-inch barrels in the new 300 Savage caliber. The 99A and 99B were also available in 300 Savage (**see Fig. 5-3**). All four of these models seem to be fairly uncommon. They are heavy due to the rifle weight barrel and probably did not sell due to the trend toward lighter weight rifles.

Table 5-1 provides simplified nomenclature that will be used in this book for the Models 1899 and 99 produced between 1899 and 1932.

Model	Characteristics 1899 to 1923
1899A	26" round barrel, solid frame
1899A TD	26" round barrel, takedown
1899A short rifle	22" round barrel, solid frame
1899A short rifle TD	22" round barrel, takedown
1899B	26" octagon barrel
1899C	26" half octagon barrel
1899D	30" round barrel musket
1899F	20" round barrel SRC
1899H	20" round lightweight barrel solid frame
1899H TD	20" round lightweight barrel takedown
1899 250-3000	22" round barrel takedown, 250 caliber@

Model	Characteristics 1923 to 1932
99A	26in round barrel, solid frame^
99B	26in round barrel, takedown^
99C	rifle weight barrel, solid frame#
99D	rifle weight barrel, takedown#
99E	lightweight barrel, solid frame#&
99F	lightweight barrel, takedown#&
99G	lightweight barrel, TD deluxe#&
99H	20in round barrel+
99K	lightweight barrel, TD engraved#&

@ There were two versions of this rifle: before WWI it had a perch belly stock and a checkered trigger; and after WWI it had a stock with a straight line from the pistol grip to the buttplate and a serrated trigger.

^ After about 1926, these rifles were changed to a 24" medium weight barrel

The barrel length of these rifles varied by caliber

& About 1926, these rifles were changed to the medium weight barrel

+ See below for the barrel changes that the 99H went through

The Savage Models 99E, 99F, and 99G

The 1899H Featherweight was replaced by the 99E, 99F, and 99G. The 99E and 99F were straight grip, uncheckered rifles in solid frame and takedown, respectively. The 99G was a takedown with a capped pistol grip and checkering and was a continuation of the second-type 1899 250-3000, except it was available in all of Savage's calibers. The barrel lengths for the 99E, F, and G were as follows: 20-inch 22 H-P, 30-30 and 303; 22-inch 250-3000; and 24-inch 300 Savage. These rifles had the lightweight barrel, but the stocks were not hollowed out, as was the case with the 1899 Featherweight. They weighed from six and a half to seven pounds (**see Figure 5-4**).

The barrels on these rifles were changed to medium weight about 1926–28. The barrel length was increased to 22 inches for 22 H-P, 30-30, and 303. The 250-3000 was continued at 22 inches and the 300 at 24 inches (**for more information on these barrel changes see the sidebar on page 67**). These later rifles with medium weight barrels were cataloged as weighing about one-quarter pound more than the rifles with the lightweight barrels. There were no other significant changes made to these models except the 99F was hand-checkered from 1938 to 1940 (**see Fig. 6-5**).

Figure 5-4. A 250-3000 99E with a 22-inch medium weight barrel (top), a 300 99F with a 24-inch medium weight takedown barrel (middle), and a 250-3000 99G with a 22-inch lightweight takedown barrel (bottom).

A Note on Variations in Rifle Weights

Regarding advertised rifle weights; a particular rifle's weight will vary some due to wood density, caliber, and barrel length. The smaller-bore rifles will weigh more because the outside diameter of the barrel is the same in all calibers, resulting in more metal left after the barrel is bored. For example, a 22 Hi-Power will weigh more than a 303 in an 1899H. A longer barrel with the same diameter bore as a rifle of the same model with a shorter barrel will weigh more. For example, an early 99G 300 Savage with a 24-inch barrel will weigh more than an early 99G 303 Savage with a 20-inch barrel. The catalogs give one weight for a model, regardless of caliber or barrel length. The weight could also vary with two otherwise identical models due to the density of the wood used in the forearm and buttstock.

The Redesigned Takedown

About 1920, the takedown barrel was changed from interrupted threads to continuous threads that required about seven turns to remove the barrel (**see Fig. 5-5**).

Figure 5-5. A 1920 and later full-threaded takedown barrel. Compare to Figures 4-11a and 4-12.

Figure 5-5a. The early takedown forearm (left) with the serial number stamped on the end. The later forearm has two wood screws securing the collar to the forearm and the serial number is stamped in the barrel channel (right).

The rear part of the takedown forearm was also redesigned. The earlier part had a transverse screw that held the metal collar onto the forearm. The wood was exposed at the rear of the forearm and the serial number was stamped there (**see Fig. 5-5a**). The new piece was solid metal across the back and two wood screws secured the collet to the forearm. They are easy to tell apart when they are on the rifle because the ends of the screw on the earlier style are visible on the sides of the collet (**see the upper forearm in Fig. 5-5b**). The serial number was stamped in the barrel channel on the new type.

Figure 5-5b. The two types of takedown forearm collars: the upper one on an 1899 250-3000 is the older style with the transverse screw; the lower one is a 99F and is the new style without the transverse screw.

The Optional 410 barrel

Savage also introduced an optional 2½-inch .410 shotgun barrel for the takedown models in 1920. It was available in 22-, 24-, and 26-inch barrel lengths, with the two shorter lengths for the lightweight F and G models (and the 99K introduced in 1926) and the heavier 26-inch for the standard weight barrel Models B and D. Savage recommended sending the rifle back to the factory to have the shotgun barrel properly fitted to the rifle's receiver. The lightweight barrels do not interchange with the standard weight barrels due to differences in the size of the channel in the forearm of the lightweight and standard weight rifles (**see Fig. 5-6**). Any 410 barrels bought separately from the rifle in the current market should be fitted by a gunsmith. All the 410 barrels were full choke. The 410 barrel did not have the forearm

lug that was used on the takedown rifle barrel; it was fitted with a bolt in a collar that screwed down against the front of the forearm to hold the forearm in place (**see the lower barrel in Fig. 5-7**). The 410 could only be used as a single shot, as the shells are too thick to fit into the rotary magazine. Medium weight .410 barrels were introduced with the changeover from lightweight to medium weight barrels in Models B, F, G, and K. Savage advertised the barrel as permitting the owner to double the use of his Model 99. He could shoot small game with it while on big game hunts and practice handling the arm by taking vermin in the off season.

Figure 5-6. A 99D forearm and 26-inch standard 410 barrel (left) and a 99G forearm and lightweight 410 barrel (right). Note the differences in width of the barrel channels and the thickness of the barrels. The taper of the lightweight barrel is also apparent.

Savage's Post— World War I Success

Savage Arms Company prospered during the 1920s and '30s, and was able to acquire a number of other arms companies, including Stevens, Fox, and Crescent Arms. This placed Savage as making the largest variety of firearms of any company in the world by the 1930s.

The Savage Combination Set

In 1921, Savage came out with a cased set featuring a Model 99G 300 Savage with a 24-inch 410 shotgun barrel in a fitted wooden case. The case was made of basswood, lined with plush blue or purple velvet, and covered with black fabrikord and nickel trim. It was called the "300 Savage Combination Kit." Some of the 410 barrels were stamped with the last three digits of the rifle's serial number. Although the catalogs say it was not available with any other style of rifle, other calibers have been observed and verified as coming from the factory with the case and 410 barrel. The engraved 99K that was introduced in 1926 has also been seen as a cased set, although it was never cataloged. The case was eventually offered separately (**see Fig. 5-7**).

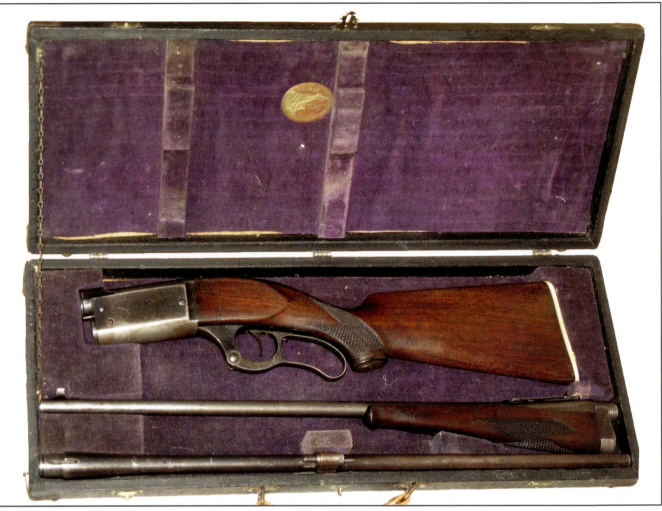

Figure 5-7. The author's "300 Savage Combination Kit" that belonged to Arctic explorer Donald B. MacMillan. The light-colored buttplate was made from walrus tusk by an unknown Inuit. Note the collar and screw on the 410 barrel that holds the barrel against the forearm.

Receiver Ring Markings

About 1920 Savage started stamping "Savage 1899 Model" on the top of the receiver ring. This practice continued into the mid-1920s, despite the fact the eighteen was dropped about 1921 and the rifles became 99A, B, C, etc. (**see Fig. 5-8**). This causes a lot of confusion among new collectors who think an early Model 99 is actually a Model 1899.

Figure 5-8. Two post-1921 receiver rings marked "Savage 1899 Model" (top) and "Savage Model 99" (bottom). The upper rifle is a 99H (serial #275983) produced in 1925. The lower rifle is a Savage 99A serial (#320964) produced in 1929.

The Savage 99H Carbine

In 1922, Savage introduced a new carbine. At first it was simply called the carbine—without a letter designation—but by 1927 it was renamed the Model 99H. There are eight variations of this rifle and the photos are grouped near the end of this section (**see Figures 5-15 to 5-17**). In the description of the carbine the Savage Arms Corporation catalog of 1922 states: "This style has the same quality barrel and action as higher priced models, but is finished in a manner making it adaptable for guides, trappers, and others desiring a sturdy, solid frame rifle for rough service, at a low price."[1] The first variation (V1-1) used a 20-inch standard rifle weight barrel and a specially designed carbine-style buttstock and buttplate (**see Figures 5-9 through 5-13**). This buttstock and buttplate were somewhat different than the earlier Savage 1899F saddle ring carbine (**see Fig. 5-9 for a comparison of the two carbine buttstocks and buttplates**).

This carbine also lacked the cheek panels on the stock just behind the receiver and the schnable forearm of the other models. It was considerably cheaper than the other 99s offered at this time as implied in the previous quote. It was initially only available in 303 and 30-30 calibers. According to the 1922 catalog it weighed seven pounds, compared to the 99E's advertised six and one-quarter pounds. Some writers say it was available with fruit wood stocks. Some of the early rifles up to 1927 have light-colored wood stocks with a dark stain, but there is no documentation from Savage (**see Figure 5-11**).

This is an interesting model, as it went through eight different variations by the time it was discontinued in 1941. See tables 5-2 and 5-3 for comparisons between the variations and Figures 5-15 to 5-17 for photos of the eight variations.

Figures 5-9. Comparison of carbine-type buttplates of a Savage 99H (left) and 1899F SRC (right).

Figure 5-11. This shows the stained light-colored wood used on some V1s. The stain is worn off, exposing the lighter wood on the upper edge of the forearm.

Table 5-2 showing the changes to make a new variation

Variations in Order of First Production

The following changes made it a new variation (each time an item changes it is noted in red):

Item	V1-1	V1-2	V2-1	V2-2	V3-1	V3-2	V1-3	V3-3
Barrel weight	Rifle	Medium	Medium	Medium	Medium	Medium	Medium	Medium
Forearm Length	11 3/16in	10 3/16in	10 3/16in	10 3/16in	10 3/16in	10 3/16in	10 3/16in	10 3/16in
Butt plate, H-carbine, or shot gun?	Carbine	Carbine	Shotgun	Carbine	Carbine	Carbine	Shotgun	Shotgun
Butt plate marking	none	none	SVG	none	none	SVG	none	Ribbed
Pads on side of stock	no pads	no pads	pads	pads	pads	pads	no pads	pads
Barrel Bands	no band	no band	brl band	brl band	brl band	brl band	no band	brl band
Front sight...ramp or dovetailed?	dovetail	dovetail	dovetail	dovetail	ramp	ramp	dovetail	ramp

Model Variation by Year and serial number range: 1st Major Variation in black, 2nd in green, 3rd in red. Additional minor variations are designated by suffixes.

Table 5-3. Model variations by year and estimated serial number range.

Year	Variation							
1922	V1-1							
1923	V1-1							
1924	V1-1	V1-2						
1925		V1-2						
1926		V1-2						
1927		V1-2						
1928		V1-2						
1929		V1-2						
1930		V1-2	V2-1					
1931			V2-1					
1932			V2-1					
1933				V2-2				
1934				V2-2				
1935				V2-2	V3-1			
1936				V2-2	V3-1	V3-2	V1-3	
1937						V3-2		
1938						V3-2		V3-3
1939								V3-3
1940								V3-3
1941								V3-3
Est.Serial Range	243xxx-265xxx	265xxx-333xxx	331xxx-340xxx	339xxx-346xxx	343xxx-356xxx	349xxx-375xxx	357xxx-358xxx	375xxx-399xxx

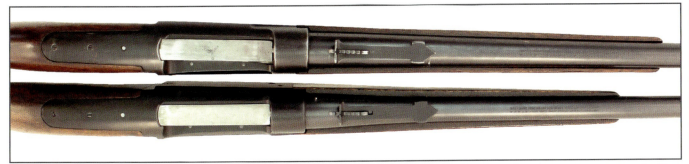

Figure 5-12. The heavier barrel and longer forearm of the V1-1 (top) compared to the V1-2 (bottom)

The information in tables 5-2 and 5-3 was compiled from observing 173 99H carbines by Rick Edmonds (Rick99 of the 24 Hour Campfire Savage forums). The smallest number observed was five for the V1-3. All other variations have at least ten examples.

In 1924, the barrel was changed to a medium weight and the forearm was shortened. This is variation V1-2. For a comparison between the V1-1 and V1-2 barrels and forearms **see Fig. 5-12. See Fig. 5-15** for an overall photo of a V1-2.

This variation was continued until 1930. The other Savage 99 models, some of which had the rifle weight barrel and others the lightweight barrel, phased in the medium weight barrel from 1926 to 1928 (**see sidebar**).

A Comparison of the Various Barrel Types Available on the Savage 1899 and 99

A good way to compare the diameter of the three barrel types is to measure the diameter of the muzzles of three 20-inch barrel rifles and carbines:

Model	Caliber	Barrel Type	Muzzle Diameter	Era of Production for the type of barrel
1899F SRC	.303	Standard	.686	1899-1926/8
1899H	.25-35	Lightweight	.567	1905-1926/8
99H (V2-2)	30-30	Medium	.632	1924-1970's

A comparison of the muzzle diameters of the Standard, Lightweight, and Medium Weight Barrels of Early Savage 99s.

All Model 99's used this medium weight barrel from the changeover in 1926–28 until the introduction of the new 99F in 1955. Some models continued with this barrel configuration into the 1970s, though the barrel diameter will vary slightly due to machining operations. The longer versions of each barrel type continued to taper and are smaller at the muzzle than the 20-inch barrel guns with the same-weight barrel. For example, an 1899A with a 26-inch standard weight barrel has a muzzle diameter of .669 inches, compared to the 1899F SRC with a muzzle diameter of .686 inches. At six inches from the muzzle (twenty inches from the rear of the barrel), the 1899A is about the same diameter as the 1899F at the muzzle.

Figure 5-13. The five types of buttplates used on the Savage 99H: left is the carbine buttplate used on V1-1, V1-2, V2-2, and V3-1; second is the V2-1 shotgun style buttplate; third is the V1-3 shotgun style buttplate; fourth is the V3-2 carbine style; and fifth is the V3-3 shotgun style buttplate.

Figure 5-14. Various sight arrangements (from left to right): first is the standard weight rifle barrel; second is the early lightweight barrel; third is the intermediate lightweight barrel; fourth is the medium weight barrel 99H V2-2 with dovetail sight; fifth is the late transition lightweight barrel; sixth is the early transition medium weight barrel; and seventh is the medium weight barrel with a long integral ramp front sight base used on most models from about 1928 until the 1950s and used on the V3-1, V3-2, and V3-3 versions of the 99H from 1935 to 1941.

In 1930, a barrel band was added near the front of a redesigned forearm, cheek panels were added to the stock, and a shotgun-style buttstock and buttplate with the SVG logo were used. These are called variation V2-1. (**See Fig. 5-16 for a photo of both V2 variations and see Fig. 5-13 for the five types of buttplates used on the various 99H models. The V2-1 buttplate is second from the left.**)

Catalog #66, which was published around 1931, said the 99H weighed six and a half pounds. Catalog #66 also shows the 99H with a barrel band and no cheek panels. There are no known carbines with a barrel band and no cheek panels. This photo continued to appear in the catalogs through #68, which was probably 1934. It was not until 1935, in catalog #69, that it was shown with cheek panels. These discrepancies in the catalogs are provided since many collectors think if the catalog shows something it has to be correct. This is not the case in many instances. The members of the 24 Hour Campfire Savage Forum (24hourcampfire.com) have compiled data from the observation of thousands of Savage Lever Action rifles and numerous historical letters to reach the conclusions I have repeated in this book.

In 1933, the 99H was made available in 250-3000. Note from the tables that shotgun buttstocks were used in the V2-1 variation from 1930 until 1932. The 99H returned to the carbine stock and buttplate in 1933 (V2-2), which continued until 1938. **(For a photo of a V2-2 see Fig. 5-16)**.

By 1935, some 99Hs had acquired the integral ramp for the front sight that was offered on other Savage 99 models since about 1926–1928. This ramp was part of the medium weight barrel package for the other models. This is the V3-1 variation **(see Fig. 5-17 for the three V3 variations)**. For the various barrel types and sight mounting options available for Savage 1899s and 99s from 1899 into the 1950s **(see Fig. 5-14)**. The rifles shown are from left to right:

- **First:** Rifle weight barrel, dovetailed front sight, Savage 99D 300 Savage serial number 252165, 1919 to 1926 barrel address, produced in 1924 (the earliest 99Hs had this weight barrel)
- **Second:** lightweight barrel, front sight base brazed in two locations, sight blade held to base with a small screw, 1899H 22 Hi-Power, serial number 123956, 1911 to 1919 barrel address, produced in 1912
- **Third:** lightweight barrel, integral front sight base, sight blade held to base with a small screw, 1899 250-3000, serial number 181752, 1911 to 1919 barrel address, produced in 1916
- **Fourth:** medium weight barrel, dovetailed front sight, 99H V2-2, 30-30, serial number 344858, barrel address 1930 to 1946 (the 99H V1-2, V1-3, V2-1, and V2-2 were the only medium weight barrel 99s to have a dovetailed front sight), produced in 1934
- **Fifth:** lightweight barrel, transition-type large integral front sight base, sight blade held to base with a small screw, 99G 303, serial number 278054, barrel address 1919 to 1926, produced in 1925

- **Sixth:** medium weight barrel, transition-type large integral front sight base, sight blade held to base with a small screw, 99G 300, serial number 290928, barrel address 1926 to 1928, produced in 1926—note this sight base is taller than number five
- **Seventh:** medium weight barrel, front sight base is a long integral ramp with a dovetail for the front sight. All previous integral front sight bases had the sight held with a screw. 99F 22 Hi-Power, serial number 328595, barrel address 1928 to 1930. Produced in 1930 (this sight setup was continued into the 1950s)

(see Appendix A for the barrel addresses cited)

Four variations of the 99H were made in 1936: the V2-2, V3-1, V3-2, and V1-3. The V3-2 had the carbine buttplate with the SVG logo and was only made in 1935 and 1936 **(see Figures 5-13 and 5-17)**. The most interesting is V1-3, which featured a shotgun butt with no panels and an unmarked buttplate **(see Fig. 5-13)**, the V1-style forearm with no barrel band, and a medium weight barrel with a dovetailed front sight. The only known examples of the V1-3 were produced in 1936 **(see Fig. 5-15)**. In 1938, the V3-3 version was introduced with a shotgun butt and ribbed buttplate with the SVG logo that was continued until the end of 99H production **(see Figures 5-13 and 5-17)**. No V3-2s have been observed after 1938. The 1939 catalog says it has a lightweight barrel and weighs six and three-quarter pounds. No 99Hs were produced with a lightweight barrel. The true lightweight barrel was phased out in all models about 1926/28. In 1940, the 300 Savage was added. The 300 Savage is the only 99H with a 22-inch barrel. Not many 99H 300 Savages were made. The other three calibers were only available with 20-inch barrels.

I grouped the photos of the eight 99H variations together so the reader can better compare them **(see Figures 5-15, 5-16, and 5-17)**. The rifles shown in **Figures 5-11 through 5-13** and **5-15 through 5-17** belong to Rick Edmonds.

The barrel band covers part of the address on some 99Hs. This has been observed on some examples of all models and calibers by Rick Edmonds **(see Fig. 5-18)**.

The 99H was dropped in 1941. It was not cataloged in 1941, although some were produced that year.

Figure 5-15. Top to bottom are V1-1 serial #262470, V1-2 serial #265884, and V1-3 serial #357982.

Figure 5-16. Model V2-1 serial #336747 (top) and V2-2 serial #346377 (bottom).

Figure 5-17. Model V3-1 serial #346754 (top), V3-2 serial #361627 (middle), and V3-3 serial #376135 (bottom).

Figure 5-18. shows the 30-30 V2-2 barrel address (top) and the partially covered address on a 300 Savage V3-3 (bottom).

The 99K

Savage introduced the 99K in 1926. It was described as a 99G with the following refinements:

Selected American walnut stock and forearm - special fancy checkering on grip, panels, and forearm. Receiver and barrel artistically engraved. Action carefully fitted and stoned. Lyman rear peep sight, folding middle sight, and raised ramp front sight base.[2]

This description is from the 1927 catalog. The rifles made in 1926 still had the lightweight barrel with the integral base front sight and a blade held by a small screw. From 1927 until the end of production the 99K had the raised ramp sight used with the changeover to the medium weight barrel. There were probably three types of front sights for the 99K. For the three types of front sights see the lightweight and medium weight barrels in **Fig. 5-14**. Some of the earliest

Ks probably had the lightweight barrel with the transition sight and the medium weight barrel with the transition sight, while most would have the medium barrel with the dovetailed ramp front sight (**see Figures 5-20 through 5-26 for photos of several 99Ks**).

The engraving varied quite a bit on these rifles. William H. Gough was an employ of Fox firearms and moved to Utica, N.Y., when Fox was purchased by Savage. He continued as an employee of Savage and did any engraving that Savage needed including the Savage Model 99K. The engraving on the upper of the two rifles in **Fig. 5-26** is deeper than the engraving on the lower rifle. The patterns also vary quite a bit. I will address these variations extensively in my book on engraved Savage 99s.

Figure 5-20. The author's Savage Model 99K serial #309466.

Figure 5-21. The exceptionally fine stock of Rick Edmonds' 99K serial #356363.

Figure 5-22. The right side of the receiver of Rick Edmonds' 99K serial #356363.

Figure 5-23. Engraving on the left side of the receiver of a Savage 99K.

Figure 5-24. Engraving on the top of the receiver and barrel on a Savage 99K.

Figure 5-25. Engraving on the lever boss of a Savage 99K.

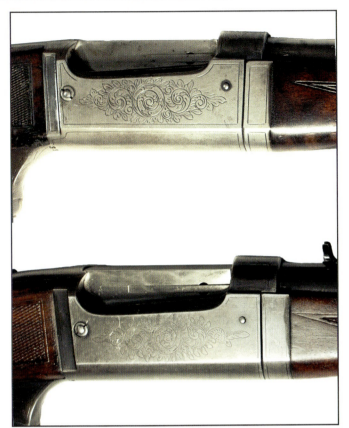

Figure 5-26. Deeper engraving on the upper 99K, compared with the lower rifle's shallower engraving. The upper rifle was made in 1930 and the lower one in 1928.

Other Changes Made About 1926 to 1932 and the End of 99C and 99D Production

The standard rifle weight barrel rifles made between 1920 and 1926 probably did not sell, judging by how few are in evidence today. Savage phased out this weight barrel between 1926 and 1928. This was also the end of 26-inch barrel production; they continued producing the 99A and 99B with 24-inch medium weight barrels and dropped the 99C and 99D from production.

About 1927/28, all Savage 99s except the 99H carbine went to an integral ramp with a 3/8-inch dovetail that held the front sight (see the sight on the far right in **Fig. 5-14**). The 99H had a 3/8-inch dovetail cut directly into the barrel for the front sight. This setup is shown fourth from the left in **Fig. 5-14**. At the same time as the change to the medium weight barrel and the ramp front sight, the 99E, F, G, and K barrels were changed to 22 inches in the 22H-P, 303, and 30-30 chamberings. The 250-3000 continued to have a 22-inch barrel and the 300 a 24-inch barrel.

The 1931 price list shows the following under the heading "Model 99 Lever Action Hi-Power Rifles": Models 99A, B, E, F, G, K, H, and Savage Combination Kit Case (only); the 410 Gauge Shotgun Barrel for Model 99 Takedown Rifles; and a Combination Kit Case Complete with Style G Rifle and 410 Barrel. Note that this no longer says 300 Savage only and probably explains the above comment about other calibers being offered in the Combination Kit option.[3]

A Rare 99G Shipping box

Dick Johnson has a 99G 30-30 in a seldom seen original shipping box. For a photo of the end of the box see **Fig. 5-27**.

Figure 5-27. The end label on the box for Dick Johnson's 99G 30-30 (serial #309389).

Barrel Addresses used from 1920 to 1946.

See **Fig. 4-32** in Chapter 4 for the standard barrel address used from 1919 to about 1926. Savage changed the barrel addresses frequently during the switch-over from the rifle weight and featherweight barrels to the medium weight barrels. They even used some featherweight barrels from the Model 1920 on the Model 99 featherweight models (see **Fig. 5-28**). There were three other barrel addresses used from 1926 to 1930 and there was probably some overlapping, at least from 1926 to 1928 (see **Figures 5-29 to 5-31**). **Fig. 5-32** shows the barrel address used from about 1930 to 1947. Some of these barrel address had a dash between N.Y. and Made. i.e. N.Y.-MADE.

Figure 5-28. This barrel address appeared on some Savage 99s about 1924. These patent dates are not for the 99, but appear on the Model 1920 bolt action rifles. They are probably lightweight Model 1920 barrels left over from that model's switch to the medium weight barrels. *Courtesy of Cheryl Johnson*

Figure 5-29. Barrel address used from about 1926–1927. *Courtesy of Cheryl Johnson*

Figure 5-30. Barrel address used from about 1926–1928.

Figure 5-31. Barrel address used around 1928–1930.

Figure 5-32. Barrel address used 1930–1946.

Chapter 6

NEW MODELS INTRODUCED FROM 1932 TO 1955

Changes Made in These Models Through 1959, WWII Production of the 99 and Savage's Involvement in the War

Trends Going into the 1930s

Judging by how few 99As, Bs, Es, and Fs are around today, it would seem that the straight grip, uncheckered rifles were not as popular as the more expensive 99G, which was checkered and had a capped pistol grip. The 99G is the model most often encountered from the 1920s and '30s.

Also of note is that Savage did not introduce any new takedowns in the 1930s. New takedowns may have been unnecessary due to the popularity of the 99G. No takedowns were produced after 1941, with the end of 99G producton.

The Savage Models 99R and 99RS

In 1932, Savage introduced the 99R and 99RS. These rifles were checkered with a capped pistol grip. The stock was heavier through the wrist and at the buttplate and had a straight forearm with a rounded end. Note in **Figures 6-1 and 6-3** the two grooves around the front of the forearm on the pre-war rifle. The postwar forearm did not have these grooves and was thicker, requiring the forearm to be tapered at the rear to match up to the receiver (**see Figure 6-4**).

The differences between the 99R and 99RS were that the 99RS had a Lyman windage and elevation adjustable rear peep sight (**see Fig. 6-2**), Lyman folding leaf middle (**see Fig. 3-9 in chapter 3**), and a gold bead front sight. It was also equipped with a 7/8-inch leather sling and quick release swivels and screw studs. The 99R was available in 250-3000

and 303 with 22-inch barrels and 300 Savage with a 24-inch barrel. The RS was not offered in 303, but was the same as the R for the other two calibers. Some 99Rs were produced in 30-30 for the A. F. Stoeger Company in the mid-1930s. In 1940, the tang sight on the RS was changed to a Redfield 70LH (**see Fig. 6-2**).

For a closeup photo of the grooves around the forearm on the 99R and RS and the sling swivel base used on pre-war 99RSs see the upper image in **Fig. 6-3**. The lower image is the quick detachable sling swivel used on the pre-war 99RS.

The great majority of 99Rs and RSs were made in the 300 Savage caliber through 1940. In 1941 and 1942, they were only listed in 300 Savage with a 24-inch barrel. No

Figure 6-1. Savage 99RS serial 388863 with the 24-inch .300 Savage barrel (top) belonging to the author and a post-WWII 99R (serial #657024) belonging to Don Johnson (bottom).

The Savage Model 99T

Figure 6-13. A Savage 99T (serial number 353421) 300 caliber from the Don Johnson collection. *Courtesy of Cheryl Johnson*

The second model introduced in 1935 was the Model 99T Featherweight, featuring a capped pistol grip, a large, wide, straight forearm, and checkering. Savage produced this rifle with special high-visibility sights and advertised it as a short, handy rifle ideal for hunting in thick woods (**see Figures 6-13 and 6-14**).

The special sights were a red bead front sight and a new semi-buckhorn rear sight without a sighting notch and with a vertical white center mark in a milled slot (**see Fig. 6-14**). For some reason very few 99Ts are found with these sights. The members of the 24 Hour Forum think many 99Ts were fitted with whatever sights were handy as the rifles came down the assembly line.

Barrel options were: 22 H-P, 250-3000, 303, and 30-30 with 20-inch barrels and .300 Savage with 22-inch barrels. The great majority of these rifles were made in 300 Savage with 250-3000 fairly rare, very few in 303 and 30-30, and 22 H-P almost nonexistent. Shortly after its introduction in 1920 and through the 1950s, the great majority of Savage 99s were produced in 300 Savage caliber. In my opinion this was because the 300 greatly outperformed all other calibers available in lever action rifles during this period. It was a proven game-getter and continues to be very effective in the hands of anyone willing to use it within reasonable ranges. (I took a cow elk at 200 yards with a 300. I would consider this to be a maximum range for elk with this cartridge.)

The Savage catalogs from 1937 (#71) to 1941 (#75) stated the Model 99 was available with either a Weaver 29-S or 330-S scope and a T7 side mount. The catalogs stated that rifles ordered with the scopes would be drilled and tapped by the factory. This was a practice continued since earliest production (**see Fig. 6-15**).

The 99T was discontinued in 1940, as Savage geared up for war production. They are fairly rare and bring a good price if they are in excellent condition. The sights pictured in Fig. 6-14 are very rare and add considerably to the price. The sights alone are very rare and also bring a high price if found separately.

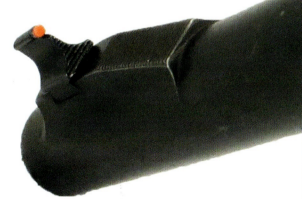

Figure 6-14. Special sights available for the Model 99T on Don Johnson's 99T.

Figure 6-15. A Savage 1899B serial #47.703 (top, c. 1904) with a Stevens #775 12X rifle scope belonging to the J. Wright collection. This configuration was available from the factory. The lower image shows a Savage Model 99T (serial #391773, 1940) with a Weaver 330-S scope and T7 mount. Unfortunately, these options never show up in Savage Historian letters.

Savage Arms' Involvement in World War II

Savage's involvement with WWII production actually began in 1939, when the maker of the Thompson sub-machine gun (Auto Ordnance Company) contracted with Savage to produce Tommy guns for the British. It was a small order at first, but increased as the war built up. Figures vary, but maybe as many as 1,500,000 were produced at the Utica plant before the end of WWII. In 1940, the US government contracted with Savage to build aircraft machine guns. Total production during the war was about 330,000, with about 15,000 being .30-caliber and the balance .50-caliber.

Early in 1941, the British contracted with Savage to produce the Lee-Enfield rifle. To have a production facility to fill this order Savage bought the New England Westinghouse factory in Chicopee Falls, Massachusetts, that was used during WWI to produce the Russian Mosin-Nagant rifle.

Over one million Enfield No.4 Mk I rifles were produced. This production came under the control of the Stevens plant, which was also in Chicopee Falls. The original Stevens plant was also used for the production of war materiel. After the US entered the war the Thompsons and Lee-Enfields were US marked and put under the Lend-Lease program. In other words, the US was paying for the production of these firearms and loaning/leasing them to the British.

Savage was always ahead of schedule and produced superior products for the war effort. The Utica plant received the Army-Navy "E" Award for high efficiency in the production of war materiel in 1942, '43, '44, and '45 (**see Fig. 6-16**). The fact that Savage was usually ahead of schedule is probably what allowed time to assemble some 99s during the war.

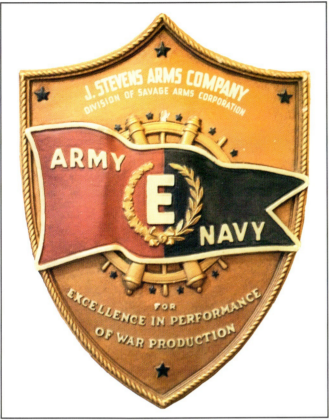

Figure 6-16. Savage's Army Navy "E" photographed at the Savage Factory. This one was presented to the Steven's Company, a division of Savage Arms Corp.

Expendable War Material Produced by Savage Arms

Savage also manufactured large quantities of parts for the weapons they produced, as well as bomb and rocket components and Springfield rifle barrels. There was an especially high need for replacement .50-caliber aircraft machine gun barrels. My father was a B-17 gunner flying out of England in 1943–44 and he said they burned up so many .50-caliber barrels they made a fence around their Quonset hut with the burned out barrels stuck vertically in the ground. They had been trained to fire short bursts to prevent the barrels from burning up, but he said they did not let off the trigger as long as a German fighter was in their sights. This practice resulted in a lot of burned out barrels that had to be replaced by Savage and other manufacturers producing .50-caliber parts.

The demand for military products decreased with the winding down of the war, resulting in most of Savage's contracts being canceled and the company finding itself with a much larger manufacturing capacity than it needed. In 1946, the decision was made to close the Utica, NY, plant and move Savage production to the Stevens plant in Chicopee Falls that had produced the British Lee-Enfield rifle. This move was accomplished and Savage brand firearms production—including the Model 99—resumed in May 1947 at the Chicopee Falls plant. Roughly 19,900 99s were produced at the Utica plant in 1946 before Savage shut down production for the move. For detailed serial number information see Appendix B.

The Savage 99 "RT"

Savage produced an interesting uncataloged variation before the move from Utica to Chicopee Falls. The members of the 24 Hour Campfire Forum refer to it as the "99RT," since it shows some of the characteristics of the 99R and the 99T. I will use this designation for clarity in any further references to the "RT." It was probably built to use up existing parts from the Utica plant. The "RT" has been observed in various barrel lengths and calibers (like 30-30) that had been discontinued prior to the date of manufacture as indicated by the serial number. The "99RT" shown in **Fig. 6-17** has EG stamped on the front of the receiver. It has a 22" 300 Savage barrel and the RT forearm. The barrel is probably a leftover 99T or 99H barrel since they had 22-inch barrels and the 300 caliber Savage EG and R had 24-inch barrels.

The "99RT's" distinguishing characteristic is a unique forearm similar to a 99T forearm, except its profile is slightly more tapered (thinner at the front) and the checkering is different than the 99T. **See Figures 6-13 and 6-17** to compare the two forearms' checkering patterns. See **Fig. 6-18** for a front view of the 99T forearm and **Fig. 6-19** for the same view of the 99RT's forearm.

This forearm may have been a prototype for the new 99R/99RS forearm (**see Figures 6-1 and 6-4**).

The changes made at Chicopee Falls to the 99EG, R, and RS are mentioned above.

Figure 6-17. Don Johnson's "99RT," serial #430504. *Courtesy of Cheryl Johnson*

Table 6-1 Lever Boss Codes for Savage 99s made from 1949 to 1968.

Letter	Year Produced	Approximate Serial Number at the First of Each Year
A	1949	520791
B	1950	5411XX
C	1951	584XXX
0	1952	625001
E	1953	663863 800,000s mostly appear in 1953-1954
F	1954	724775
G	1955	758274 some 900,000s appear in late 1955
H	1956	7731XX
I	1957	927489
J	1958	949XXX
K	1959	9593XX
L	1960	968395 post mil rifles started in 1960 with serial number 1,000,000
M	1961	1014XXX
N	1962	1037000
P	1963	1052XXX
R	1964	1070711
S	1965	1085XXX
T	1966	1109XXX
U	1967	1113XXX
V	1968	116XXXX The "A" series of serial numbers started in December 1968. See Appendix 2 for these production figures.
W	1969	A009045
X	1970	A387575
Y	1971	A667385

Figure 6-18. Front view of a 99T forearm.

Figure 6-19. The "99RT" forearm showing the sharper taper. The 99T forearm also has a different style of checkering than the 99T

The Savage 99's Lever Boss Code

In 1949, Savage started stamping a code in a small oval on the front of the lever boss. The oval contained one or two numbers that identified the inspector, followed by a letter that designated the year the rifle was produced. The letters O and Q were skipped to avoid confusion. The designations ended at Y and the letter Z was not used (**see Table 6-1 and Fig. 6-20**). In some cases these codes were lightly stamped, making it difficult or impossible to read the date code. These serial numbers are derived from various forum members pooling information from the rifles that they have observed.

Savage stopped stamping the rifle's serial number on the fore end, buttstock, and buttplate in 1950, replacing it with an assembly code that was not related to the serial number. This assembly code is stamped on the receiver's lower tang and the forearm, buttstock, and buttplate. It is necessary to remove the buttplate, buttstock, and forearm to see these codes.

Figure 6-20. Lever boss code 16I on Savage 99F, serial #943592. The 16 is the inspector's code and the I indicates the rifle was produced in 1957.

The Savage 99F

In 1955, Savage introduced a new Savage Model 99F Featherweight. It was the first new model since the introduction of the 99EG and 99T in 1935 and featured the first true lightweight barrel since the 99Es, Fs, Gs, and Ks were changed from a lightweight to a medium weight barrel about 1926/28 (**see Figure 6-21**).

The forearm was thin and featured a rounded end. The barrel was 22 inches long and had a raised barrel boss with a dovetail for the rear sight (**see Figure 6-22**). This barrel type was also used on the 99DL, PE, DE, and early 99Cs, except for these models chambered in 284 Winchester. These models and the 284 cartridge will be covered in Chapter 7.

The lever was slimmed and the buttstock hollowed out to reduce weight (**see Fig. 6-23**).

The right side of the barrel was marked "Model - 99F" just under the "Hi-Pressure Steel – Proof Tested" marking

in front of the receiver (**see Fig. 6-22**). This was the first time Savage marked a 99 with a letter designation in this manner. Previous to this the letter designation was stamped on the front of the receiver on some rifles (many did not have the designation stamped on them), requiring the forearm be removed to see the letter designation.

The 1955 catalog claimed a weight of six and one-half pounds and it was offered in 250-3000 and 300 Savage calibers. These calibers are listed in the 1956 to 1959 catalogs, along with 243, 308, and 358 Winchester. Most 99Fs starting with serial number 900,000 were produced in the Winchester calibers. The 99F was the only Chicopee Falls Savage 99 continued in production at Westfield, Massachusetts, and changes to the 99F after the move to Westfield will be covered in Chapter 7.

Figure 6-21. A Savage 99F (serial #764405), 300 Savage caliber belonging to the author. The sling swivels on this rifle were cataloged in the Savage catalogs of this era (1955) and could have been factory installed.

Figure 6-22. The Savage 99F rear sight and dovetailed barrel boss. The rear sight was changed to the folding model in 1959 (see Fig. 7-2).

Figure 6-23. The 99F hollowed-out buttstock and corrugated steel buttplate. The assembly code is visible on the buttstock.

Sorting Out Confusing Model Designations

There is a point of confusion concerning Savage 99 designations. Starting in the early 1920s and continuing into the early 1940s, Savage produced rifles designated Models 99A, B, C, D, E, F, G, H, and K (**see Chapter 5 for information on these rifles**). All of these rifles were discontinued by the beginning of World War II. Starting in 1955 with the 99F, Savage recycled some of these designations. They also reused 99E, C, and A over the next twenty years. They also used 99CD, which was actually an 1899 designation for a checkered, pistol grip variation for rifles made from 1905 to about 1917 (**see Chapter 4 for more information on the 1899CD**). For the rest of the book I will use the designations 99A prewar, 99A postwar, etc., if there is any possibility of confusion within the context of the subject being addressed (**see Table 6-2 for a brief description of the differences**). For more detail on the individual models see the appropriate chapter.

Table 6-2 A brief comparison of Savage 99s with the same letter designations.

Old Model

Designation	Characteristics
99F pre-war	Lightweight/medium weight TD barrel. Straight grip, unchecked stock except 1938–1940 is checkered (see Chapter 5).
99E pre-war	Lightweight/medium weight solid frame barrel, unchecked stock, cartridge counter (see Chapter 5).
99C pre-war	Rifle weight solid frame barrel, straight grip, unchecked stock, rotary magazine, cartridge counter (see Chapter 5).
99A pre-war	Rifle weight solid frame/later medium weight barrel, straight grip unchecked stock (see Chapter 5).
1899CD	Checkered pistol grip available with rifle weight 1899A, B, C, short rifle, lightweight round 1899H. Solid frame and takedown available (see Chapter 4).

New Model

Designation	Characteristics
99F postwar	Lightweight barrel with boss for rear sight, capped pistol grip stock with checkering and hollowed out buttstock (see Chapters 6 and 7).
99E postwar	Economy model, straight tapered barrel, early unchecked, later impressed checkered fruitwood stock, no cartridge counter (see Chapter 7).
99C postwar	Lightweight later straight tapered barrel, pistol grip impressed checkered/later laser checkered stock, removable clip magazine, no cartridge counter (see Chapter 7).
99A postwar	Straight tapered barrel, unchecked straight grip stock with Schnabel forearm (see Chapter 7).
99CD postwar	Deluxe, straight tapered barrel, hand-checkered Monte Carlo stock with cheekpiece and recoil pad (see Chapter 7).

Savage 99 30-06 Prototype

During the 1930s, Savage produced a prototype Savage 99 in 30-06 Government caliber. The label on the rifle displayed at the Savage factory says it was the only Savage 99 High Powered rifle built (**see Fig. 6-24**). For details on why this rifle was not put into production see the interview with Ronald Coburn in Chapter 8.

Figure 6-24. Savage 99 prototype 30-06. Note the extra long action and unique lever and safety.

A Cutaway Savage 99EG

Rick Edmonds has an interesting cutaway 99EG that is shown in **Figures 6-25 and 6-26.**

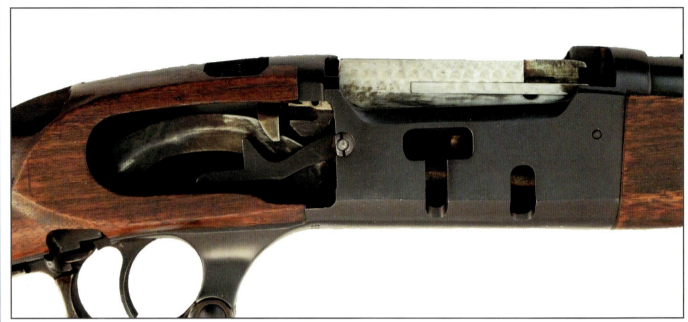

Figure 6-25. The right side of Rick Edmonds' cutaway Savage 99EG with the lever closed. The hammer is in the uncocked or safe position.

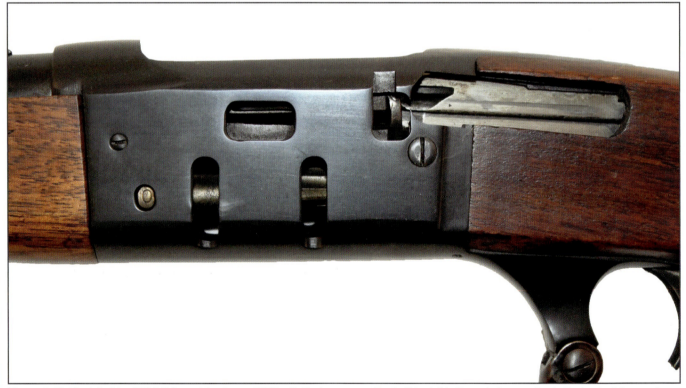

Figure 6-26. The left side of Rick Edmonds' cutaway 99EG with the lever open. The bolt is visible through the opening in the back of the receiver and the stock's cheekpiece. The rotary magazine is visible through the vertical slots in the lower receiver.

Barrel Addresses Used from 1930 to 1960

The barrel addresses used from 1930 to 1946 are shown in **Fig. 6-27** and 1947 to 1960 are shown in **Fig. 6-28**.

Figure 6-27. The Savage 99 barrel address used from 1930–1946. Some rifles have a long "–" between "N.Y." and "MADE" in the lower line.

Figure 6-28. The Savage 99 barrel address used 1947–1960.

Chapter 7

WESTFIELD, MASSACHUSETTS, PRODUCTION 1960 TO 2003

The Move from Chicopee Falls to Westfield, Model 99s Listed in the 1960 Catalog, and the First Post-Mil 99E

The factory was moved to Westfield, Massachusetts, in 1960. The last of the 99EGs and 99Rs were produced in Chicopee Falls.

Two new models (99DL and 99E) were introduced and the 99F underwent the changes given below with the move to Westfield. The 1960 catalog and the price list dated January 7, 1960, still have the Chicopee Falls address. The catalog shows the 99F and the new 99DL with gold triggers and tang safeties. These rifles were produced at the Westfield plant and have serial numbers above 1,000,000. Serial number 1,000,000 was a one-off custom presented to the NRA and will be covered in detail in my book on engraved and special order Savages. I will refer to the 99s with serial numbers below 1,000,000 as pre-mil and those above 1,000,000 as post-mil for the remainder of the book. The 99EG and 99R were discontinued prior to the factory being moved to Westfield in 1960. The 1960 catalog pictures the 99R and says the EG is still available. The price list shows a picture of the 99R, but not the 99EG. The catalog shows a 99E that looks like the 99EG without checkering or a pistol grip cap. This rifle is shown with a plastic buttplate and is listed in the price list. It was only available in 300 and 250-3000 Savage and the catalog states it has a 24-inch barrel and cartridge counter. Very few of these rifles are known to exist. Under the 99E entry the catalog states the 99-EG is available and is similar to the 99E, with the following features: "Checkered pistol grip and fore-end, damascened bolt, capped pistol grip, and corrugated steel butt plate."[1,2] The 99EG had been available in the Winchester calibers for the last few years, but the catalog says it only differed from the 99E with the features quoted above. I am sure the EGs and Rs were cataloged to sell off any remaining stock of these models that were produced at Chicopee Falls and that EGs in the Winchester calibers still would have been available. If any of these rifles were produced in 1960 they would have lever boss code "L." None are known to exist. The 99DL, 99F, and 99R are listed as being available in 300 and .250-3000 Savage, 308, 358, and 243 Winchester.[3]

The rate of the rifling twist in the 250-3000 was changed from 1 turn in 14 inches to 1 in 10 at this time. This change allowed bullets of 100 grains to stabilize which improves accuracy with this weight bullet. At about this time the threads on the barrel and receiver were changed from a square design to a "V" shape.

The Savage 99DL

The new 99DL featured a 24-inch lightweight barrel with the raised boss at the rear sight, a folding rear sight, a Monte Carlo stock with studs for quick detachable sling swivels, aluminum buttplate, tang safety, and the gold trigger, plus a new sear that allowed for a crisp trigger pull. The new sear was a stamped part. Its design did not allow the trigger to be held down to decock the rifle when the lever was closed. The model designation on the left side of the receiver ring is "Savage Model 99M." The "M" stands for Monte Carlo and this designation also appears on the Models 99DE and 99PE that were introduced in 1965. See Fig. 7-1 for a photo of an early Savage 99DL and Fig. 7-2 for the folding rear sight used on the DL and 99F. This sight was first available on the 99F in 1959. See Fig. 7-3 for the aluminum buttplate used on the 99DL.

Figure 7-1. An early Savage 99DL 358 Winchester caliber with a 24-inch barrel and hand checkering. This rifle is from the J. Wrigh collection. *Photographed at Savage Fest 2014 by Charlotte Roya*

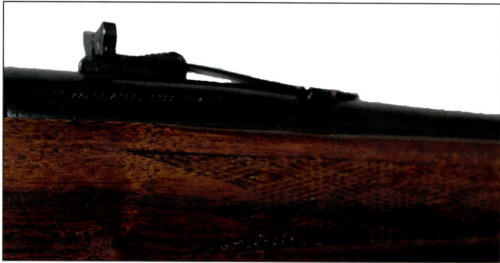

Figure 7-2. The folding rear sight used on the 99F and 99DL. This is a 99DL in 284 Winchester caliber and does not have a boss where the rear sight is mounted due to the thicker, straight-tapered barrel. The 284 caliber was introduced in 1964.

Figure 7-3. The aluminum buttplate used on the 99DL edge of the buttplate was unpainted and shows as a silvery edge.

The Post-Mil Savage Model 99F

The 99F continued unchanged, except for the tang safety and gold trigger and the new sear that was part of the tang safety package. Due to the location of the tang safety it was no longer drilled and tapped for a tang sight. The popularity of rifle scopes had been increasing significantly during the 1950s and this feature may not have been missed much due to the fact that rifle scopes were replacing peep sights as the more accurate alternative to open sights.

The New Savage 99E

Figure 7-4. Early 99E with the stained fruit wood stock

The 1961 catalog lists the 99F and 99DL unchanged from 1960, except that the .250-3000 caliber was no longer offered. The 99E is listed as "New for 61."[4] It is listed with a 24-inch barrel in 300 Savage and a 20-inch barrel in 243 and 308. The barrels are medium weight. The stock is listed as walnut finish, meaning it was stained fruit wood. The stock continued to be unchecked through 1965. Starting in 1966 it had stamped checkering. It had the hard rubber buttplate continued from 1960. This rifle did not have a cartridge counter, making it the first 99 not to have one. It had a lever safety, but the tang was not drilled and tapped for a tang sight. The catalog entry stresses the rifle was a no frills economy model, but with the dependability of the more expensive models. They are not very attractive but are accurate. I have shot consistent three-shot one-inch groups with several 99Es in 308 (**see Fig. 7-4 for a photo of an early 99E**).

By 1963, the 99DL was listed with a 22-inch barrel. From this point on it and the 99F were the same, except for the Monte Carlo stock and aluminum buttplate on the DL as opposed to a stock with a straight line across the top and corrugated steel buttplate used on the 99F. The buttstock was not hollowed out on the DL. The DL was no longer cataloged in the .358 caliber after 1964.

Introduction of the 284 Winchester Cartridge and Modifications to the Model 99 to Handle this Cartridge

Figure 7-5. A stamped checkered Savage 99 DL in 284 Winchester. It is serial #1091424, LBC T, produced in 1966.

In 1964, the new 284 Winchester cartridge was introduced in the 99DL and 99F. The catalog failed to mention that due to the larger diameter of this cartridge the rotary magazine held only four rounds. There was also a major redesign of the tension adjustment for the rotary magazine on the 284. This redesign eliminated the need for the tension screw that is near the front of the receiver on the other caliber rifles. The 99E in **Fig. 7-4** clearly shows the end of the tension screw. The 284 in **Fig. 7-5** does not have the tension screw. For a comparison of the two tension adjusters on rifles with the forearms removed **see Fig. 7-5a**. Note the 284 has a circlip to hold the tension adjuster in place. The 284s have a stronger medium weight straight tapered barrel, probably necessary to handle the larger diameter of this cartridge and the higher pressures generated. This larger diameter made the boss at the rear sight unnecessary. This was the last year for hand checkering on these models, making a hand-checkered 284 DL or F a one-year-only rifle. In 1965, Savage followed the rest of the American firearms industry by replacing hand-checkered stocks with inexpensive-looking stamped checkering. The patterns varied some from year to year and model to model, but in my opinion were of a low quality not in keeping with the quality of the rest of the rifle. Ron Coburn told me this change was necessary because the Savage factory was unable to find enough employees with the dexterity to cut the fine lines required for hand-checkering and not mess up the whole stock. He also told me that a drawback to stamped checkering was the upper and lower dies could not adjust for the natural variations that come with hand-sanded wood, resulting in checkering that was often shallow on one end and too deep on the other. (**See Fig. 7-5 for a stamped checkered DL in 284 Winchester.**)

This rifle and a 99E in my possession are good examples of Savage not producing 99s in sequential order by serial number. The lever boss codes indicate the DL was produced in 1966 and the 99E was produced in 1965, however, the serial number on the DL is 1091424 and the 99E's serial number is 1105344. Due to the difference between the 284 receiver and the other calibers Savage may have made a large run of 284 receivers at the beginning of availability of that caliber and then used them as there was demand. Ron Coburn advised me that the Bureau of Alcohol, Tobacco, and Firearms requires that once a firearm receiver is complete it has to be stamped with a serial number; the ATF considers it a firearm and the serial number allows it to be tracked through the assembly process. The 284 receivers would have been stamped with the serial number when they were produced and the LBC applied when the rifle was finished.

This ruling dates to before WWII. Savage was given a special dispensation during WWII to serialize the firearm after it was fully assembled and tested for both proof and

Figure 7-5a. Comparison of a rotary magazine 284 tension adjuster to a regular Model 99 tension adjuster.

function so that the manufacturing process could go faster and only functional guns had sequential numbers.

Historian letters have revealed other rifles that were produced later than their serial numbers would indicate. I have an 1899F serial number 192035 that would indicate late 1917 production, yet the historian letter says it was sent to the shipping department in August 1919. There are probably a number of explanations for rifles that were shipped out of order.

Introduction of the Savage Model 99C

Figure 7-6. An early Savage Model 99C with the lightweight barrel. Serial #1100778 caliber 308 from the Don Johnson collection.

The year 1965 also saw the introduction of three new models. The most radical was the Savage 99C. It featured a four-round detachable magazine (three rounds in .284). This was the first major departure from the receiver's design since the model 1895 was introduced. The bottom of the magazine was rounded to conform to the shape of the bottom of the receiver. The calibers offered in the 99C were 243, 284, and 308 Winchester. It had a recessed button on the right side of the receiver that released the magazine. There were no cartridge counters on the 99Cs. **See Fig. 7-6** for an early 99C and **see Fig. 7-7** for a closeup of a 99C receiver and its magazine. All caliber bullets except 284 fit the standard magazine, which is usually marked 243/308.

The photo in the 1965 catalog shows a tapered medium weight barrel without the rear sight boss. From 1966 until 1972, the catalogs show the rear sight boss that was a feature of the lightweight barrel. Possibly the 1966 and 1973 catalogs show a .284 that would not have the boss. The early 99Cs that I have observed in calibers other than 284 have the lightweight barrel with the sight boss. Some 99Cs could have been produced with the straight tapered barrel in the other calibers. The 99C was available until the end of Savage 99 production in 2003. Many of the changes it went through were also incorporated in the other models. I will treat the changes to the 99C as they occur through the remainder of this chapter.

Figure 7-7. The 99C with the magazine removed. Note the magazine release button on the side of the receiver and the word "front" written top to bottom on the magazine. Three magazines are shown: the top one is in position to be inserted into the receiver, the middle one is oriented to show the follower, and the third shows how the magazine looks with one round loaded.

Other Changes Made Over the Next Few Years

Starting in 1965, the 99DL was no longer listed as being chambered in 358 Winchester. The 99F continued to be the only 99 offered in this caliber through 1968. From 1969 through 1976, no 99s were offered in 358. Rick Edmonds mentioned in his review of this section that Savage did make some rotary magazine rifles in 358 in 1974. These may have come out of Savage Services. They did the repairs on rifles returned to the factory and may have made up uncataloged variations, such as these 358s. It is a good idea if the reader comes up with something odd like this that he seek a Savage historian letter on the rifle.

The Engraved Savage Models 99PE and 99DE

In 1965, Savage also introduced two new engraved models: the 99PE Presentation Grade and 99DE Citation Grade. These were the first regular production engraved rifles since the 99K was discontinued before WWII. These rifles were basically a fancy 99DL. The receivers were marked Model 99M, indicating they had a Monte Carlo stock, and they were equipped with an aluminum buttplate like the DL. The more expensive of the two (99PE) had a mountain lion engraved on the right side of the receiver, an elk on the left, and floral engraving on the bottom. The coverage of the engraving was more extensive than the DE and it featured "very select" hand-checkered walnut stocks. The 99DE had floral engraved ovals on each side of the receiver with a deer on the bottom. The DE had pressed checkered "select" walnut stocks. The receivers on both rifles were left in the white and were finished with a clear protective coat.

It is a shame that Savage had to ruin the "select walnut" stock on the DE with pressed checkering, which was necessary due to the unavailability of skilled workers to do hand checkering (**see Figures 7-8 through 7-13**).

The engraving varies some on these rifles. Most notably there is an Eastern version of the PE with deciduous trees in the background and a Western version with evergreens in the background. The two examples below are the Western version. Some rifles had more detail and deeper engraving, such as the lower of the two 99PEs pictured in **Figures 7-12 and 7-13**.

Models 99 PE and DE do not have a lever boss code and were equipped with a small folding rear sight (**see Fig. 7-14 for the small rear sight that appeared on these rifles, as** **well as some of the other Savage 99 models**). Elevation adjustments were accomplished by loosening the two screws and sliding the small centerpiece up or down as necessary. Windage adjustments required drifting the sight in the dovetail.

There were no other changes made to these rifles other than variations in engraving until they were discontinued in 1970. The engraving on these models will be covered in more detail in my book on engraved Savage 99s. The rifles shown in **Figures 7-8 through 7-14** are in the author's collection.

Figure 7-8. A Savage Model 99PE (top) and 99DE (bottom).

Figure 7-9. A Savage 99DE; both sides were essentially the same engraving.

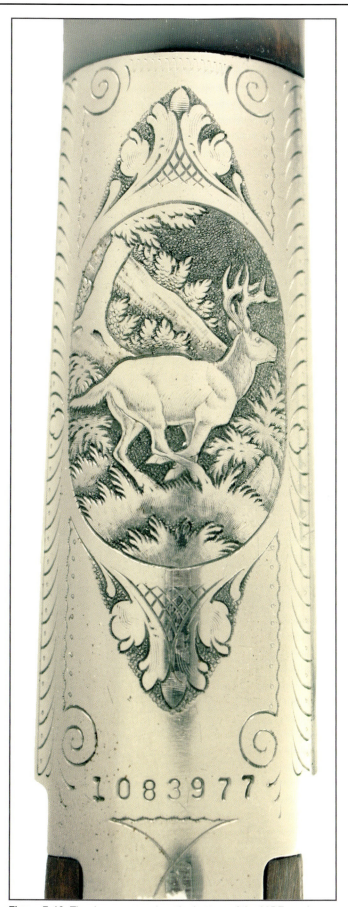

Figure 7-10. The deer engraved on the bottom of the 99DE receiver

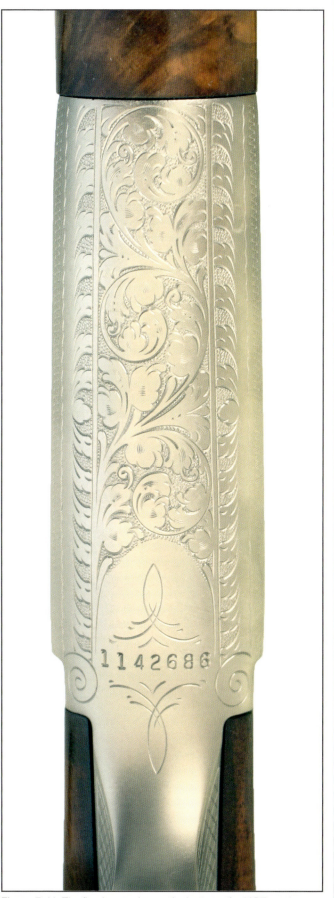

Figure 7-11. The floral engraving on the bottom of a 99PE receiver.

Figure 7-12. This photo and Fig. 7-13 show more detail and deeper engraving on the lower PE than on the upper. The upper rifle is a .243, serial #1142686. The lower PE is a .284, serial #1139589.

Figure 7-13. The Right side of the 99PEs' receivers.

Figure 7-14. The small folding rear sight used on many Savage 99s in the 1960s and '70s, including the 99PE and 99DE. This rifle is a 284 with the straight tapered barrel and does not have a barrel boss for the rear sight.

The Savage Brand Rifle Scope and the Savage Model 99E/S

Savage introduced a line of rifle scopes, mounts, and rings in 1963 and pictured various Model 99s with a scope mounted. These scopes are very clear and appear to be of fairly high quality. Starting in 1967, they listed a 99E with a scope package and called it the 99E/S. This package included a 4X scope, rings, and bases. This scope would have been the Model 0433 or 0433P (post) made by Suwa of Japan. The E/S had a folding rear sight, while the 99E continued with a sporting rear sight with the step elevator. By buying this package the buyer could save almost 50% on the cost of the scope (**see Fig. 7-15**). For closeups of the scope see **Fig. 7-16**. Although it is not visible in the photo, the rings were marked "Savage, Westfield, Mass., USA."

Figure 7-15. Savage 99E/S caliber .308, serial #1181317.

Figure 7-16. A Savage model 0433B scope (upper) and the manufacturer's identification (left).

The New Alphanumeric Numbering System

Nineteen sixty-eight was the first year for a new serial numbering system. The serial number was moved from the bottom of the receiver to the left side and consisted of a letter and six digits (**see Table 7-1**). All of Savage's production was consecutively numbered. This system does not assign any range or block of numbers to any particular model, meaning the serial numbers of center fire rifles, rimfire rifles, and shotguns were serial numbered in the order they were produced.

Alphanumeric Serial Numbers by Production Date

Table 7-1 Years of Manufacture for Savage Model 99 from 1968 to 1998.

Serial Number at the First of Each Year[5]

Month	Year	Serial Number
12-16-1968	1968	A001001
Jan	1969	A009045
Jan	1970	A387575
Jan	1971	A667385
Jan	1972	A949195
Jan	1973	B256621
Jan	1974	B437451
Jan	1975	B792306
Jan	1976	C086746
Jan	1977	C349146
Jan	1978	C627156
Jan	1979	C943702
Jan	1980	D284936
Jan	1981	D633026
Jan	1982	D889826
Jan	1983	E083636
Jan	1984	E219801
Jan	1985	E415511
Jan	1986	E597296
Jan	1987	E715586
Jan	1988	E900721
Jan	1989	E970341
Jan	1990	F039711
Jan	1991	F102731
Jan	1992	F161501
Jan	1993	F214401
Jan	1994	F284901
Jan	1995	F396381
Jan	1996	F512681
Jan	1997	F600441
Jan	1998	F677441

Savage historian John T. Callahan provided me with the following information from his records: the "F" serial numbers ended in November 2001, while the "G" serial numbers started in December 2001 and finished in November 2009. 99C production ended in 2003.[6]

The Savage 1895 75th Anniversary Commemorative

In 1970, Savage celebrated their seventy-fifth anniversary with a commemorative Model 99 called the 1895 75th Anniversary Commemorative. The label on the box says it is an exact copy of the 1895, but it varies quite a bit from the original 1895s. It was chambered in 308 Winchester with a 24-inch octagon barrel. The 1895s were all .303 Savage and were available with several barrel lengths, but not 24 inches. The 75th Commemorative has some engraving on the sides of the receiver, a brass medallion inletted on the right side of the buttstock, and a brass-plated lever and crescent buttplate. These features also vary from the original 1895. It does have a lever safety. With the exception of the 99E, the other Model 99s made in 1970 had tang safeties. Ten thousand were produced in 1970, which was the only year of manufacture. Some owners who have fired their 75th Commemoratives say they are very accurate due to the heavy 24-inch barrel (**see Figures 7-17 through 7-19**). Production for the 99PE and 99DE ended in 1970.

A small quantity of 99Cs exists with octagon barrels. It is assumed these were assembled using leftover 75th anniversary barrels (**see Fig. 7-20**). Quite a few such anomalies have been observed in Savage 99s over the years. I have kept pretty much to standard production features in this book. If the reader finds a rifle that seems to vary from the features in this book, I would recommend going to the 24 Hour Campfire Savage Forum and asking about the rifle; it is always best to post photos with the enquiry.

Figure 7-17. A 75th anniversary commemorative.

Figure 7-18. Engraving on the right side of the receiver of the 75th anniversary commemorative.

Figure 7-19. Engraving on the left side of the receiver of the 75th anniversary commemorative.

Figure 7-20. Rick Edmonds' Savage 99C with a 24-inch octagonal barrel in .308 (serial #C387192) produced in 1977.

The New Savage Model 99A

A new model (Model 99A) was introduced in 1971. It featured a straight grip stock for the first time since the 99F (pre-war) and 99H were discontinued in 1940/41. It had a Schnabel fore end, was uncheckered, and had a steel buttplate. It was offered in 250-3000 (back by popular demand, according to Savage's advertising), 300 Savage, 243, and 308. It had a 20-inch straight-tapered barrel, tang safety, and cartridge counter. Savage advertising called it a saddle gun and stressed the nostalgic aspect of the gun. The 99A shown in **Fig. 7-21** is caliber 375 Winchester, which is very scarce. For more on the 375 caliber see the section on the brush gun.

Figure 7-21. A Savage 99A (postwar), serial #D676721, caliber 375 Winchester produced in 1981.

Changes that Occurred in the Early to Mid-1970s

Starting in 1971, the 99DL was no longer offered in 300 Savage and the 99F was listed as having a blued trigger. The 99F was also listed as having an aluminum buttplate. However, the photos used in the catalogs continue to show it with a steel buttplate through the end of production in 1973. In 1972, the C is the only 99 offered in 284. The 99E/S is no longer listed in the 1973 catalog and no scopes are listed. The 99DL and 99F are no longer listed in the 1974 catalog and the 99C is no longer listed in .284. This is the end of Savage 99s produced in 284 Winchester. It is also the end of production for the lightweight barrel. At this point, the 99C shared the straight tapered 22-inch medium weight barrel with the other Savage 99 models.

To summarize: By 1974, the only model 99s listed were the 99C, 99E, and 99A. The 99C was listed in 243 and 308; the 99E in 300 Savage, 243, and 308; and the 99A in 250-3000, 243, and 308. The 99C had a 22-inch barrel and the E and A had 20-inch barrels. The 99A and 99E went to 22-inch barrels in 1976. All three models had straight tapered barrels until the end of production.

The Savage 99CD

In 1975, Savage introduced the 99CD. This was a deluxe detachable magazine model. It had a number of firsts for the Savage 99 line: a thin rubber recoil pad; a Monte Carlo stock with a cheekpiece; and a thick beavertail fore end with finger grooves. It also came standard with a sling and swivels, a new Williams rear sight that was windage and elevation adjustable, a new hooded front sight, and hand checkering. The hood was large and must have been unpopular, as it is very seldom seen on the rifles that originally came with it. The rifle pictured in **Fig. 7-32** has the hood on the front sight. These sights became available on the other models in 1981. The bottom of the forearm was checkered. The stock was described as select walnut with a deeply fluted comb (**see Figures 7-22 to 7-24**).

Figure 7-22. A Savage 99CD. This is a prototype that was kept at the factory until 1981. It is in caliber 250 and the serial number is RD278. The author bought it from Dick Johnson in 2014.

Figure 7-23. Checkering on the bottom of the 99CD forend.

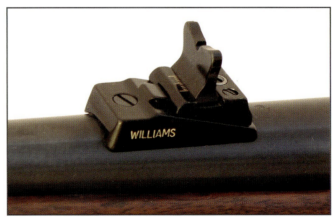

Figure 7-24. A Williams rear sight used on the 99CD.

The Introduction of the 22-250 Remington Cartridge and Changes that Occurred in the Late 1970s

In 1977, Savage started offering the 22-250 Remington caliber in the 99C. This caliber was only available for three years and these rifles are very scarce. My 99C 22-250 consistently shoots one inch and under groups. The 99 in this caliber did not catch on with the varmint and long range shooting crowds because their bolt action rifles with their longer, heavier barrels did not heat up as quickly as the 99's barrel, giving better accuracy. However, it is fitting that the 99 was offered in 22-250, since the smaller cartridge was developed by necking the 250-3000 Savage cartridge down to .224-inch. **See Fig. 7-25** for a photo of the 99C 22-250.

This rifle is a good example of the appearance of the 99C throughout the 1970s. It looked almost as plain as the 99E, although it had walnut stocks and a cap on the pistol grip. The small folding leaf rear sight is the same sight that was offered on the 99PE and DE and is shown in **Fig. 7-14**.

Figure 7-25. A Savage 99C 22-250. This rifle is serial #D133898, produced in 1979.

The Savage Model 99-358 and 99-375 (Brush Gun)

Figure 7-26. The author's 99-358 (bush gun), serial #C699374, produced in 1978.

Figure 7-27. The heavy duty recoil pad on the 99-358.

In 1977, Savage introduced what was to be their last new model 99: the Model 99-358, commonly called the Brush Gun. It had a straight-grip uncheckered stock with a heavy beavertail forend and finger grooves, a 22-inch barrel, and a thick recoil pad (**see Figures 7-26 and 7-27**).

Introduction of the 375 Winchester Cartridge and Changes in the Early 1980s

In 1980, Savage added 375 Winchester to this line, cataloged as the Model 99-375. The 358 continued to be available. The 1980 catalog shows it with a thinner, non-ventilated recoil pad. This was the last year for Brush Gun production. The rifle in either caliber is scarce and brings a pretty good price in today's market.

The 1980 catalog shows the 99C with the heavy grooved forend and cut checkering. The 99C and 99CD were only offered in 243 and 308 in 1980.

By 1981, the 99CD and Brush Gun (99-358 and 99-375) were discontinued. The 99A was available in 375 as well as 250-3000, 243, and 308, and was the last model to have a cartridge counter.

Introduction of the 7mm-08 Cartridge and Changes to 1984

In 1981, caliber 7mm-08 was introduced in the 99C. The 99C had taken on all the characteristics of the 99CD, except it did not have a cheek piece and the recoil pad was thicker (**see Figures 7-22, 7-28, and 7-29**).

Figure 7-28. The 1981 version of the 99C. This particular rifle is caliber 7mm-08.

Figure 7-29. The only differences between the 99CD (top) that was discontinued in 1980 and the 1981 version of the 99C is that the 99C does not have the cheekpiece and has a thicker recoil pad.

The End of Rotary Magazine Production and Changes in the Savage Model 99C Until the End of Production

Savage did not put a date on their catalogs for the next few years. The one that is about 1983–84 shows only the 99C and 99E. The 99A was discontinued before 1983. The 99C is unchanged from the rifle in **Fig. 7-28**. The 99E now has a thick forearm with the finger grooves and was offered in 250-3000 Savage as well as 300 savage, 243, and 308. It also had a cartridge counter in 1983–84. Savage was probably using up the last receivers from the other rotary magazine models.

The End of Rotary Magazine Production— the Savage Model 99C is the Only 99 Continued in Production

Starting about 1985, the only 99 offered was the 99C. The 99E was the last of the rotary magazine rifles and was probably discontinued at the end of 1984. The 99C was only offered in 243 and 308. The forearm had returned to a thinner beavertail style without the finger grooves and the buttstock and forearm were laser checkered (**see Fig. 7-30**).

Savage was in bad shape financially by the mid-1980s. Fortunately, Ronald Coburn became CEO shortly after this and managed to pull the company out of bankruptcy (**for more on Ronald Coburn and the end of 99 production see Chapter 8**). No Model 99s were produced from about 1987 to 1991.

Figure 7-30. The last version of the 99C (serial #F836211), produced in 1999.

The Spanish-made Llama Savage Model 99

About 1992, Savage contracted with the Llama arms manufacturer in Spain to make a Savage 99C and shipped all remaining receivers and small parts to Llama. About a thousand were produced and it was in its own serial number range, starting with L1000 and running to about L2100/ L2200. The Llamas were the only 99s produced with an L prefix on the serial number. It was available in 243 and 308,

although few 243s were produced. Many of the rifles had to be reworked at the Savage factory and the contract was canceled (**see Figures 7-31 to 7-32**).

Savage started producing the Model 99C again at the Westfield plant probably about 1995–1996. This rifle was very similar to the Llama. Compare the rifle in **Fig. 7-30** that was produced in 1999 with the Llama in **Fig. 7-32**.

Figure 7-31. Box end label for Rory Reynoldson's Llama 99C, showing it is .308 caliber and serial number L1810.

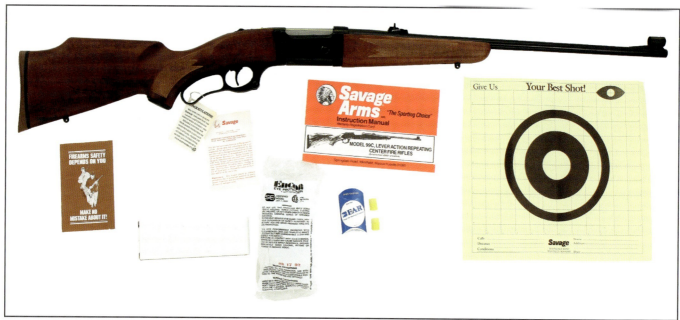

Figure 7-32. A Spanish Llama-produced 99C with the paperwork that accompanied it. This rifle is new in the box and belongs to Rory Reynoldson.

The 100th Anniversary Commemorative and the Rocky Mountain Elk Foundation Commemorative

The 99C was the only regular model manufactured until the end of production. Along with the regular production models there were two commemoratives produced using the 99C action: the 100th Anniversary Commemorative produced in 1996 (**see Figures 7-33 to 7-35**) and the Rocky Mountain Elk Foundation Commemorative produced in 1998 (**see Figures 7-36 to 7-39**). Both rifles were offered in 300 Savage only. These rifles were the first detachable magazine 99s offered in 300 Savage.

The Savage Model 99CE 100th Anniversary Commemorative was announced in 1996. The original intent was to manufacture 1,000, but shortly after the model was announced Ron Coburn told me Savage received orders for more than that figure. They produced about 1,800 to fill the demand. It came with a fitted wooden box that was lined with a soft cotton material that was recessed to fit the profile of the rifle. The serial number was on the bottom of the receiver in the pre-1968 location and had the prefix AS. The serial numbers started at AS0001 and were sequentially numbered to the end of production (**see Figures 7-34 and 7-35 for closeups of the engraving and the gold inlay animals on the receiver**). The engraving is similar to the 99PE (**see Figures 7-9 and 7-10**). Only sixty RMEF rifles were produced. (**see Figures 7-36 and 7-39**)

Figure 7-33. Savage's 100th anniversary commemorative produced in 1996.

Figure 7-34. The right side of the 100th anniversary commemorative's receiver.

Figure 7-35. The left side of the 100th anniversary commemorative's receiver.

Figure 7-36. A Savage Model 99C Rocky Mountain Elk Foundation commemorative belonging to the J. Wright collection.

Figure 7-37. The right side of the receiver of the J. Wright collection's RMEF 99.

Figure 7-38. The left side of the receiver of the J. Wright collection's RMEF 99.

Figure 7-39. The bottom of the receiver of the J. Wright collection's RMEF 99.

The Last 99s Produced and the End of 99 Production

The regular production 99C was never cataloged as being offered in 300 Savage, but a few were produced in this caliber around 1999. These probably had leftover barrels from the 100th Anniversary and Rocky Mountain Elk Foundation commemoratives. The 100th anniversary model had a special barrel address (**see Fig. 7-44**). The regular production Savage 99C and the RMEF rifle had the standard barrel address (**see Fig. 7-47**).

Although 1997 was the last year Savage cataloged the 99, they continued to offer the 99C in 243 and 308 until 2003. A few were produced (probably more accurate to say they assembled a few) in the G serial number range.

Barrel Addresses Used from 1960 to 2003

The barrel addresses for 1960 to 2003 Savage 99s are shown in **Figures 7-40 to 7-47**.

Figure 7-40. The barrel address used in the 1960s.

Figure 7-41. Brush Gun 358 series A barrel marking. This is a good example of '70s and '80s barrel markings for all 99s, with the exception of the Model 99C. The caliber was part of the barrel address.

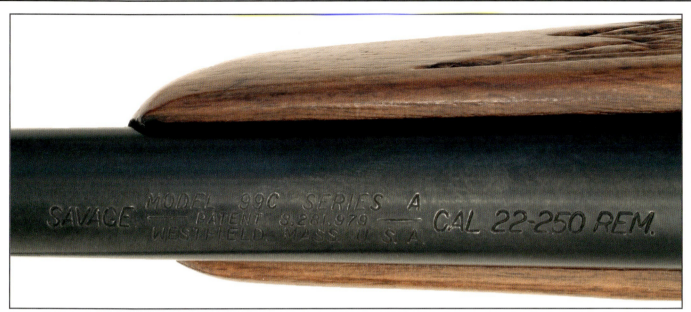

Figure 7-42. An example of the barrel addresses used on 99Cs in the 1970s and 1980s. Note the patent number for the 99C modification is part of the barrel address as well as the caliber.

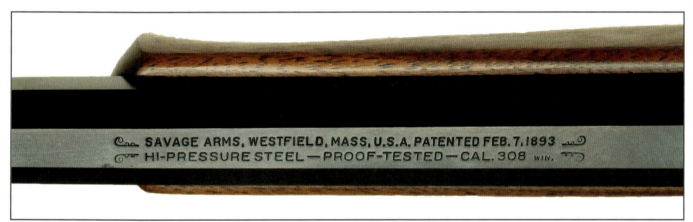

Figure 7-43. The Model 1895 75th anniversary barrel address. This used the February 7, 1893, patent date and the squiggles at the beginning and ending of each line similar to the 1895 barrel address. Compare to **Fig. 2-21**.

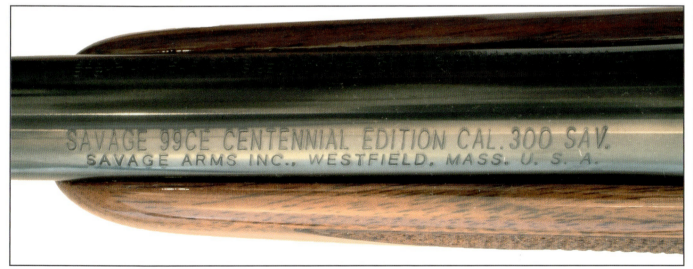

Figure 7-44. The Model 99CE 100th Anniversary barrel address.

Figure 7-45. The left side barrel address on the Model 99C produced by Llama.

Figure 7-46. The Llama's right side barrel address.

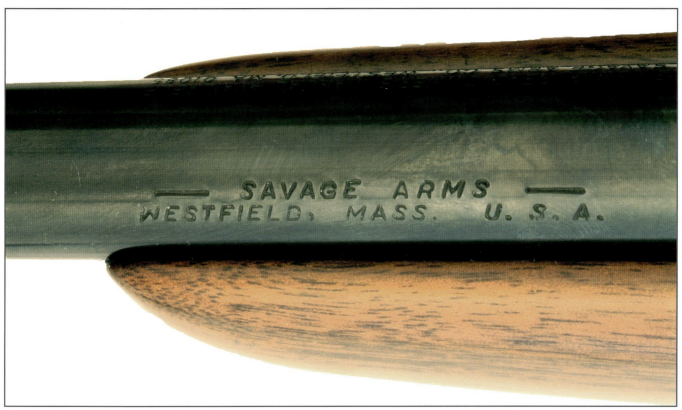

Figure 7-47. The RMEF and late-production barrel address. There is a warning on the right side of the barrel. The caliber marking was on the left side of the barrel, near the receiver.

Chapter 8

RONALD COBURN AND THE AUTHOR'S FINAL WORD

Figure 8-1. Ronald Coburn and his wife, Barbara; Ron is holding the Savage 99PE .308 that he hunts with. Some of Barbara's art is hanging on the wall behind them.

While I was making the appointment to visit the Savage factory I asked Ronald Coburn's former secretary, Kathy Thomas, if Ron was still in the area, and if so would it be possible for me to get in touch with him. Ronald Coburn had retired as CEO earlier after twenty-five years with the company. He is credited with pulling the company out of bankruptcy shortly after he took over in the late 1980s. Ron

called me a few days later and made an appointment for us to spend the day with he and his wife, Barbara (**see Fig. 8-1**).

Ron Coburn's Collection of Savage 99s

Ron had his collection of Savage Lever Action Rifles out for us to photograph (**see Figures 8-2 through 8-12**).

Ron is a native of Ireland and immigrated to the United States many years ago. He first entered the firearms industry in the US by going to work for Smith & Wesson in 1980 as director of engineering. He next worked for Case Cutlery in Bradford, Pennsylvania, which he turned around financially and ultimately sold to Zippo Lighters, another well-known company in the same town. In 1988, Ron joined Savage as vice president in charge of operations shortly before the company filed for bankruptcy in 1988. A month into bankruptcy Ron took over as CEO. With a lot of support from Barbara (who thought he was crazy) he turned the company around. This required a lot of cost-cutting measures, including laying off most of the employees and cutting Savage production back to only two centerfire rifles: the 99 and the bolt action Savage Model 110. The company was profitable and growing under Ron's leadership by 1995. The owners then decided to sell to Mossberg. Ron realized the company was about to get shaken up again. He was able to raise the money and bring in partners to make the owners the same deal Mossberg was offering. The owners sold the company to Ron and his partners. The company was thriving by 2012 and the partners decided to go public. ATK bought the company. Ron decided to retire in early 2013 and pursue other interests. The company is still going great. They produced more centerfire rifles in 2013 than any other American firearms manufacturer.

Figure 8-2. Ronald Coburn's 1895 octagonal barrel rifle. Note the rare shotgun style buttstock and buttplate.

Figure 8-3. Ronald Coburn's 1899 round barrel rifle. Note the special-order pistol grip.

Figure 8-4. Ronald Coburn's 1899's pistol grip. Note the curved lever. The earlier rifles with pistol grips had the same straight lever as the rifles without pistol grips, such as the engraved rifle on the cover of the book.

Figure 8-5. Ronald Coburn's custom 99, a highly embellished 99PE (see Figures 8-6 through 8-9).

Figure 8-6. The left side of the rifle's receiver in Fig. 8-5.

Figure 8-7. The right side of the rifle in Fig. 8-5.

Figure 8-8. The bottom of the receiver and lever of the rifle in Fig. 8-5.

Figure 8-9. The top of the rifle's receiver in Fig. 8-5.

Figure 8-10. Ron Coburn's 99PE.

Figure 8-11. Ron Coburn's 99CE.

Figure 8-12. Ron Coburn's 1895 75th Anniversary Commemorative.

Why the Savage Model 99 was Discontinued

A question on a lot of people's minds is why the Savage 99 is no longer produced. As in most things there were many reasons. First of all, people's tastes change. Even in the 1950s, when Savage produced a large number of 99s, more people were switching to bolt action rifles. This trend continues today. While the bolt rifles are still popular, semi-automatics are getting a larger and larger share of the market. This trend had progressed until lever action rifles only had a small following, meaning the market for a lever action rifle is small. Low production numbers equate to a higher manufacturing cost per rifle.

Another trend is toward more powerful rifles. Ron had his engineers explore the possibility of redesigning the 99's action to handle more powerful cartridges. The area where the bolt engages the rear of the receiver has a four-degree angle that allows the bolt to drop down when the action is opened (**see Fig. 8-13**). If this area was straight up and down the action would not open. This necessary angle makes for

an area of weakness. The bolt will disengage when ammunition of higher pressures than the 308 Winchester class of ammo are fired in the 99. To overcome this difficulty would have required a radically new design that would not have had much resemblance to the beloved Savage Model 99.

The biggest problem was one of assembly. The action of the 99 is fully enclosed within the receiver, meaning if a rifle does not work properly after final assembly the action has to be taken completely apart, the parts suspected of being the problem honed, and the action reassembled. Ron said this procedure had to be repeated as many as five or six times to get some rifles to function properly. About one in five functioned correctly after the initial assembly. In today's world of high cost for skilled labor there was no way to continue producing the Savage Model 99.

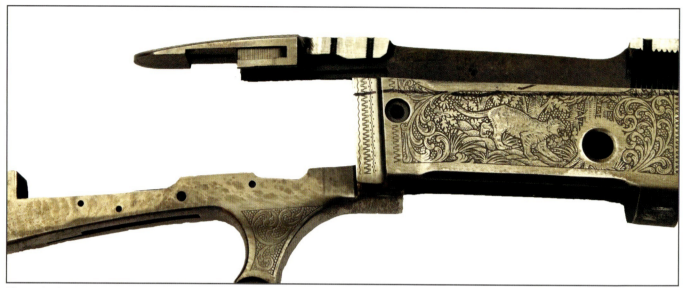

Figure 8-13. A cutaway Savage 99C receiver showing the four degree angle on the rear of the receiver, where the bolt mates to the receiver when the bolt is closed.

The Author's Final Word on the Savage 99

Figure 8-14. The author's sixty-year-old Savage 99EG (serial #727750). This rifle was in the earliest batch of EGs that were factory drilled and tapped for scope mounting.

Am I saddened by the cessation of production of the 99? Somewhat. But we have to be realistic. It was an extremely innovative piece of machinery 119 years ago. Keep in mind that automobiles were not much more than dreams of forward-thinking individuals in 1894 when Arthur Savage perfected the design of the Model 1895 and founded the Savage Repeating Arms Company and technology has progressed since then. The 1895 was invented and produced when some hand fitting was the norm and skilled labor was relatively inexpensive. Today CNC machinery cranks out a perfect product that can be put together and shipped out to the consumer with minimal handling by human beings and is therefore inexpensive. The design of the Savage 99 is such that it requires some hand fitting.

Does this obsolescence mean the Savage Model 99 is no longer capable of taking wild game and should only be hung on the wall? Not hardly. See **Fig. 5-2** for a photo of a caribou I killed with a 64-year-old 99R in October 2014. In 2014, Ron Coburn took a moose with a Savage 99 .300. There are a number of people still hunting with the venerable 99, including many members of the 24 Hour Campfire Savage forum. The Savage 99 looks good hanging on the wall, too—when you are not out hunting with it (**see Fig. 8-14**).

David Royal

THE SAVAGE MODEL 1895, 1899, AND 99 BARREL ADDRESSES

The barrel addresses are repeated here for ease of reference. Barrel addresses used from 1895 to about 1926 are shown in **Figures A-1 to A-5**. Note the earliest 1899 barrel address (**Fig. A-2**) is identical to the 1895 barrel address (**Fig. A-1**), except the word "Repeating" is left out. This was due to the Company's name change from Savage Repeating Arms Company to Savage Arms Company in 1897. All of the Marlin-produced 1895s use the barrel address in **Fig. A-1** and have the "M" or "JM" stamp on the underside of the barrel.

Figure A-1. The Savage Model 1895 barrel address

Figure A-2. The early Savage Model 1899 barrel address used from 1899 to about 1904.

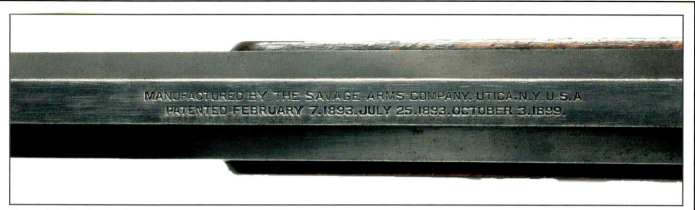

Figure A-3. The Savage Model 1899 barrel address used from about 1904 to 1911.

Figure A-4. The Savage Model 1899 barrel address used from about 1911 to 1919.

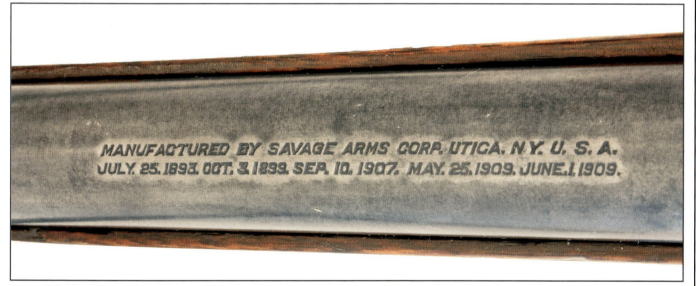

Figure A-5. The Savage Model 1899 and Model 99 barrel address used from 1919 to about 1926.

Some of the lightweight Model 99s were produced with leftover lightweight Model 1920 barrels. The patent dates appearing on the barrel are for the Model 1920, not the Model 99 (**see Fig. A-6**).

Figure A-6. The Savage Model 99 barrel address seen on some lightweight models produced around 1926.

The barrel addresses used from about 1926 to 1930 appear to overlap somewhat (**see Figures A-7 to A-9**): **Fig. A-7** is on a lightweight barrel; **Fig. A-8** is on a medium weight transition barrel; and **Fig. A-9** is on a late-1920s medium weight barrel.

Figure A-7. The Savage Model 99 barrel address used around 1926 to 1927.

Figure A-8. The Savage Model 99 barrel address used around 1926 to 1928.

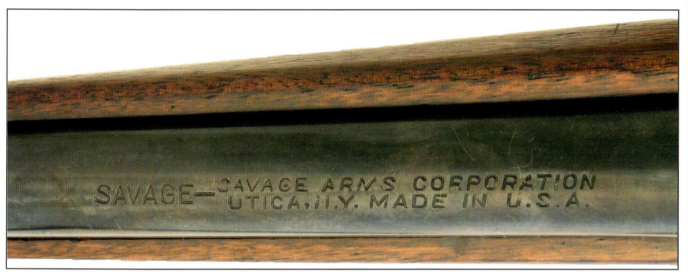

Figure A-9. The Savage Model 99 barrel address used around 1928 to 1930.

Savage used the same barrel address from 1930 to 1946, when production ended at the Utica plant (**see Fig. A-10**). A similar barrel address was used throughout Model 99 production at the Chicopee Falls, Massachusetts, plant from 1947 to 1960 (**see Fig. A-11**). There are some post-mil rifles that have this address. These rifles were produced in Westfield and probably used leftover barrels from Chicopee Falls production.

Figure A-10. The Savage Model 99 barrel address used from 1930 to 1946. Some barrel addresses in this era had a dash between N.Y. and MADE, i.e. N.Y.-MADE.

Figure A-11. The Savage Model 99 barrel address used from 1947 to 1960.

The early Westfield, Massachusetts, rifle had the barrel address shown in **Fig. A-12**.

Figure A-12. The Savage Model 99 barrel address used from 1960 to probably the early 1970s.

The 75th Anniversary Model 1895 had a unique barrel address that used the 1895 patent date and the symbols at the beginning and end of each line of script in the original 1895 barrel address. **Compare Figures A-1 and A-13.**

Figure A-13. The Model 1895 75th Anniversary Commemorative barrel address.

Around the early 1970s Savage started calling the rifles Series A and incorporated that designation and the caliber into the barrel address (**see Fig. A-13a**). The 99C's barrel address also included the patent number for the detachable magazine version of the action (**see Fig. A-14**).

Figure A-13a. An example of Series A type barrel addresses used on the rotary magazine models from about the early 1970s to the early 1980s. This one is on a Model 99-358 Brush Gun. Each type series A barrel address shows the caliber of the particular rifle.

Figure A-14. The barrel address used on the 99Cs and CDs showing the patent number for the detachable magazine rifle used from about the early 1970s to the early 1980s.

The barrel addresses for the remainder of Model 99C production are shown in **Figures A-15 to A-18**.

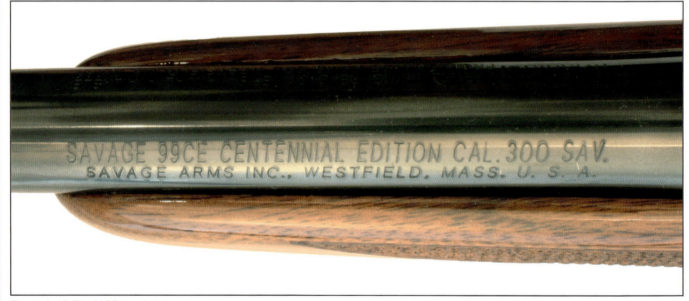

Figure A-15. The 99CE barrel address.

Figure A-16. The barrel address used on the left side of the Llama 99C's barrel.

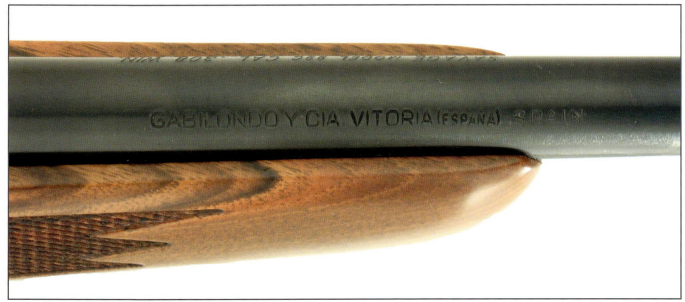

Figure A-17. The barrel address used on the right side of the Llama 99C's barrel.

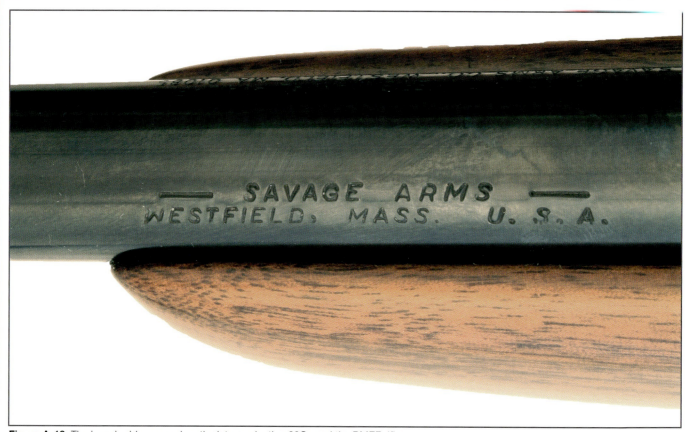

Figure A-18. The barrel address used on the late production 99Cs and the RMEF rifle.

DATES OF MANUFACTURE OF SAVAGE 99 RIFLES

The 1895s were manufactured by Marlin. The serial numbers ranged from the low 3000s to the low 8000s. My round barrel 1895 (serial number 7844) letters as being produced in 1896, even though its serial number places it in the last 400 or 500 Model 1895s produced. Marlin probably made a run of them in 1895 and 1896 and then Arthur Savage sold them over the next four years.

The Savage Model 1899s and 99s were not produced in strict sequential order. The following information gives a ballpark idea on when they were produced. The Historical Department at Savage Arms now provides letters on Savage firearms. Their address is: Savage Arms, Historical Department, 100 Springdale Road, Westfield, MA, 01085.

The following table is reproduced from Jay Kimmel's *Savage & Stevens Arms.*[1] It covers Savage 1899 and 99 production from 1898 to 1940.

Table B-1 Production Figures for Savage Models 1899 and 99 From 1899 to 1940

Year	Serial Number	Quantity
1898	unknown	unknown
1899	unknown	unknown
1900	11501-13400	1900
1901	13401-19500	6100
1902	19501-25000	5500
1903	25001-35000	10000
1904	35001-45000	10000
1905	45001-53000	8000
1906	53001-67500	4500*
1907	67501-73500	6500
1908	73501-81000	7500
1909	81001-95000	14000
1910	95001-110000	15000
1911	110001-119000	8000
1912	119001-131000	12000
1913	131001-146500	15500
1914	146501-162000	15500
1915	162001-175500	13500
1916	175501-187500	12000
1917	187501-193000	5500
1918	Production suspended - WWI@	
1919	193001-212500	19500
1920	212501-229000	16500
1921	229001-237500	8500
1922	237501-244500	7000
1923	244501-256000	11500
1924	256001-270000	14000
1925	270001-280000	10000
1926	280001-292500	12500
1927	292501-305000	12500
1928	305001-317000	12000
1929	317001-324500	7500
1930	324501-334500	10000
1931	334501-338500	4000
1932	338501-341000	2500
1933	341001-344500	3500

* It appears as though no 1899s were produced with serial numbers between about 55,000 and 64,900.

1934	344501-345800	1300
1935	345801-350800	5000
1936	350801-359800	9000
1937	359801-370000	10200
1938	370001-381350	11350
1939	381351-388650	7300
1940	388651-398400	9750

@a few 1899s were probably produced in 1918

The production dates are continued until 1945 in David O. Moreton's *The Savage Story.*[2] Moreton's table did not include the number produced; I added those figures to the table.

Table B-2 Savage Model 99 Production From 1941 to 1945

Year	Serial Number	Quantity
1941	398401-409980	11580
1942	409981-421190	11210
1943	421191-423040	1850
1944	423041-425700	2660
1945	425701-427700	2000

A footnote with Jay Kimmel's table (Table B-1) states that serial number 447601 was the last rifle shipped from Utica and that it was shipped October 11, 1945. Production continued in Utica in 1946, and I believe that date should be late 1946, with a production figure for that year of about 19,900. I arrived at this production figure by subtracting Moreton's ending number 427,700 in 1945 (Table B-2) from Kimmel's figure 447,601.

Savage 99 production in Chicopee Falls started with serial number 500000 in 1947; in other words, there are no Model 99s with serial numbers between about 447601 and 499999. About 4,000 99s were produced in 1947 (serial numbers 500,000 to about 504xxx). About 16,000 were produced in 1948 (serial numbers from about 504xxx to 520,790). The rifles produced in 1948 and probably some produced in 1947 had an asterisk stamped on the lever boss.

In 1949, Savage started stamping an oval on the front of the lever boss that contained two numbers indicating the inspector and a letter indicating the year the rifle was produced. As mentioned in Chapter 6, a receiver was stamped with the serial number when the receiver was produced. Apparently the lever boss code was stamped when the rifle was actually assembled, giving a more accurate picture of when the rifle was finished. The lever boss codes are listed in Chapter 6 and reproduced in Table B-3.

Table B-3 Lever Boss Codes Showing Savage 99 Production Dates from 1949 to 1971

Letter	Year Produced	Approximate serial number
A	1949	520791
B	1950	5411XX
C	1951	584XXX
D	1952	625001
E	1953	663863 800,000's mostly appear in 1953-1954
F	1954	724775
G	1955	758274 some 900,000 appear in late 1955
H	1956	7731XX
I	1957	927489
J	1958	949XXX
K	1959	9593XX
L	1960	968395 post mil rifles started in 1960
M	1961	1014XXX
N	1962	1037000

P	1963	1052XXX
R	1964	1070711
S	1965	1085XXX
T	1966	1109XXX
U	1967	1113XXX
V	1968	116XXXX The "A" series of serial numbers started in December 1968. See Appendix 2 for these production figures.
W	1969	A009045
X	1970	A387575
Y	1971	A667385

In 1968, Savage went to an alphanumeric serial numbering system that numbered all firearms produced in sequence; Model 99s, other centerfire rifles, rim fires, and shotguns were serial numbered as they were produced. (The serial numbers used at the beginning of each year appear in Chapter 7 and Table B-4.)

The last Savage Model 99s produced had a G prefix. Savage historian John T. Callahan provided me with the following information: the "F" serial numbers ended in November 2001. The "G" serial numbers started in December 2001 and finished in November 2009. Of course, 99C production ended in 2003. The last 99s were shipped in 2003.

As noted in Chapter 7, the Spanish Llama models had a serial number starting with an "L" and were numbered sequentially, as they were not produced at the Savage factory. These serial numbers were from L1000 to a little higher than L2000.

Table B-4 The Alphanumeric Serial Numbers by Year Produced Serial Number at First of each Year

Month	Year	Serial Number	Month	Year	Serial Number
12-16-1968	1968	A001001	Jan	1984	E219801
Jan	1969	A009045	Jan	1985	E415511
Jan	1970	A387575	Jan	1986	E597296
Jan	1971	A667385	Jan	1987	E715586
Jan	1972	A949195	Jan	1988	E900721
Jan	1973	B256621	Jan	1989	E970341
Jan	1974	B437451	Jan	1990	F039711
Jan	1975	B792306	Jan	1991	F102731
Jan	1976	C086746	Jan	1992	F161501
Jan	1977	C349146	Jan	1993	F214401
Jan	1978	C627156	Jan	1994	F284901
Jan	1979	C943702	Jan	1995	F396381
Jan	1980	D284936	Jan	1996	F512681
Jan	1981	D633026	Jan	1997	F600441
Jan	1982	D889826	Jan	1998	F677441
Jan	1983	E083636			

The last Savage Model 99's produced had a G prefix. No information is available on when this series was started. The last 99's were shipped in 2003.

CALIBERS AVAILABLE IN THE SAVAGE MODELS
1895, 1899, and 99 by Years Produced and Model

There are two ways I have organized this appendix. First, I chose "by caliber" for several reasons. The rifles are all marked by caliber, making that a good place to start identifying a rifle. The collector can check the caliber and then go to the appropriate chapters to compare the rifle to the photos and specifications. Second, if the collector wants to find a rifle in a specific caliber he can quickly see the models made in that caliber and the year(s) produced (see Table C-1). Table C-2 lists the rifles by model and shows the calibers available for that particular model. In some cases I combined models that were made at the same time and in the same calibers together. Not all models were available in all calibers during their production run. To identify when a particular model was available in a given caliber refer to table C-1.

Table C-1 Models listed by caliber

Caliber	Models Available in This Caliber	Approximate Dates Available
303 Savage	1895	1895 - 1899
	All 1899's	1899 - 1920
	99	1921 - 1940 (available in all models except the 99RS)
30-30 Winchester	1899	1902 - 1920
	99	1921 - 1940 (available in all models except the 99R and 99RS)
25-35 Winchester	All 1899's	1903 - 1917
32-40 Winchester	1899	1903 - 1917 (available in all models except the 1899H)
38-55 Winchester	1899	1903 - 1917 (available in all models except the 1899H)
22 Savage Hi-Power	1899H takedown	1912 - 1920
	99E, F, G, K, EG, T	1921 - 1940
250-3000 Savage	1899 250-3000	1914 - 1920
	99E, F, G, K, EG, T	1921 - 1961
	99A	1971 - 1981
	99CD	1975 - 1979
	99E	1983 - 1984
300 Savage	All 99's	1921 - 1959
	99F	1955 - 1973
	99DL	1960 - 1970
	99E	1960 - 1984
	99A	1971 - 1973
	99CE	1996
	99RMEF	1998
	99C	1999
308 Winchester	All 99's	1956 - 2003 (the 99CE and 99C RMEF were the only 99's not made in 308 during this period)
243 Winchester	All 99's	1956 - 1974
	99A, C, and E	1975
	99A, C, CD, and E	1976 - 1980
	All 99's	1981 - 2003
358 Winchester	All 99's	1956-1959
	99F and DL	1960 - 1964
	99F	1965 - 1968
	99-358 Brush Gun	1977 - 1980

284 Winchester	99DL	1964 - 1969
	99F	1964 - 1970
	99 DE and PE	1965 - 1970
	99C	1965 - 1972
22-250 Remington	99C	1977-1979
375 Winchester	99-375Brush Gun	1980
	99A	1981 - 1982
7mm-08 Remington	99C	1981-1984

Table C-2 Calibers listed by model

Model	Calibers Available
1895	303 Savage
1899A, A short rifle, B, C, F, and CD	303 Savage, 30-30, 25-35, 32-40, and 38-55 Winchester
1899H	303, 30-30 and 25-35
1899H takedown	22 Savage Hi-Power, 303, 30-30 and 25-35
1899 250-3000	250-3000 Savage
99A, B, C, and D	303, 30-30, 300 Savage
99E, F, G, K, and T	22H-P, 250-3000, 303, 30-30, 300
99H	303, 30-30, 250-3000, 300
99R	250-3000, 303, 300, 243, 308, 358
99RS	250-3000, 300, 243, 308, 358
99EG	22H-P, 250-3000, 303, 30-30, 300, 243, 308, 358
99F	250-3000, 300, 243, 308, 358, 284 Winchester
99DL	250-3000, 300, 243, 308, 358, 284
99E	250, 300, 243, 308
99C	300, 243, 308, 284, 22-250 Remington, 7mm-08 Remington
99DE, PE	243, 308, 284
99A	243, 250, 300, 308, 375 Winchester
99CD	243, 250-3000, 308
99-358	358
99-375	375
99CE	300
99 RMEF	300

SOME VINTAGE PHOTOS OF PEOPLE WITH THEIR SAVAGE RIFLES

Gary Groshel (a.k.a. Groghel Deluxe on the 24 Hour Campfire Savage Forum) has collected vintage photos of people, their guns, and their trophies for many years. He kindly let me use some of them in this book.

Native Trout caught near Cody, Wyo.

8/23/37

#165

EXPLORER CHECKS BISQUICK FOR REDFERN TREK: Theodore Waldeck, veteran explorer, lecturer and motion picture expert, shown as he made a final check on his food supply before shipping it to his headquarters in Georgetown, British Guiana, South America. Accompanied by Mrs. Waldeck, he will penetrate the fastnesses of unexplored jungle country on a ten-months' search for Paul Redfern, American aviator lost in 1927. Real home-baked biscuits, says Waldeck, are an important and luxurious diet item for both explorers and native porters on long wilderness trips.

256-3

ENDNOTES

Chapter 1

1. Bailey Brower, Jr. *Savage Pistols* (Mechanicsburg, Pennsylvania: Stackpole Books, 2008), pp 4–10.

Chapter 2

1. *Savage Repeating Arms Co.,* catalog, Utica, NY, June 1895, p 16.
2. Luke Mercaldo. *Allied Rifle Contracts in America.* (Wet Dog Publications, 2011, Greensboro, NC) pp190–194.

Chapter 3

1. Savage Arms Co., catalog, Utica, NY, 1900, p 15.
2. Savage Arms Co. catalog 1900, p 54.
3. Ibid. p 26.
4. Savage Arms Co. catalog No. 15 (1905) pp 29–32.

Chapter 4

1. *Savage Arms Company,* 1903 Catalog, p 48.
2. Private correspondence between the author and Blair Power.
3. *Savage Arms Company,* Catalog No. 15, pp 29–32.
4. Douglas P. Murray. *The Ninety-Nine, Revised Third Edition.* (Westbury, NY, 1985) pp 3–22 to 3–23.
5. *Savage Arms Co.,* Catalog No. 24, p 16B.
6. *Savage Arms Co.,* 1912 catalog p 6 and 1912 price list.
7. *Savage Arms Co.,* Catalog No. 55 c. 1916, p 1.
8. Mercaldo, op.sit., pp 195–203.
9. Private correspondence between the author and Blair Power.
10. Copies of letters from the various parties involved made available to the author by Blair Power.

11. Mercaldo, op.sit., p 207.

Chapter 5

1. *Savage Arms Corporation,* catalog #63 dated 1922, p 13.
2. *Savage Firearms and Ammunition* catalog, small format, no date or number. Some of the 99s pictured have the 1925/1926 transition type front sight. This would place the catalog about 1926.
3. *Savage Retail Price List Effective January 15, 1931.*

Chapter 6

1. *Savage Arms Corporation,* catalog #32-50, 1950, p 4.

Chapter 7

1. *Savage Stevens Fox rifles and shotguns,* 1960, p 3.
2. *Savage Arms Corporation Dealer Price List, Effective January 7, 1960,* p 2.
3. *Savage Stevens Fox rifles and shotguns 1960,* pp 2 and 3.
4. *Savage Stevens Fox Shotguns and rifles* 1961, p 3.
5. This information was provided to the author by Rick Edmonds from the *Red Savage Parts Book.* This information only goes to January 1998.
6. Personal correspondence between John T. Callahan and the author.

Chapter 8

No end notes for Chapter 8

BIBLIOGRAPHY

Brower Jr., Bailey. *Savage Pistols*. Mechanicsburg, Pennsylvania: Stackpole Books, 2008

Mercaldo, Luke. *Allied Rifle Contracts in America*. Greensboro, North Carolina: Wet Dog Publications, 2011

Murray, Douglas P. *The Ninety-Nine*. Westbury, Long Island, New York: Douglas P Murray, 1985.

Kimmel, Jay. *Savage & Stevens Arms, Collector's History, Fifth Edition, 1864–2003*. Portland, Oregon: CoryStevens Publishing, Inc., 1990